Epics describe anecdotes in unique way. The anecdotes eulogize lord Vishnu as the protector for species in their path to trod for becoming ionized spirits. The process of ionization of spirits to fuse into lord the Almighty, goes on from *time immemorial*. The species have aligned themselves to the culture of *fission-fusion* forever subjected to whimsic invisible force, remaining dormant, as Maya. The species, as such, undergo transformation in a cycle, elevation to depression and vice-versa.

18 Purans in Diamond Pocket Books

Shiv Puran
Vishnu Puran
Markandeya Puran
Bhanishya Puran
Narad Puran
Shrimad Bhagvat Puran
Devi Bhagvat Puran
Garud Puran
Agni Puran
Kalki Puran
Ling Puran
Varah Puran
Bhrahamevart Puran
Vayu Puran
Padma Puran
Harivash Puran
Ganesh Puran
Brahma Puran

Padma Purana

Dr. Vinay

DIAMOND BOOKS

ISBN : 81-288-1748-5

© Publisher

Published by	: **Diamond Pocket Books Pvt. Ltd.**
	X-30, Okhla Industrial Area, Phase-II
	New Delhi-110020
Phone	: 011-41611861-65, 40712100
Fax	: 011-41611866
E-mail	: sales@dpb.in
Website	: www.dpb.in
Edition	. 2018
Printed by	: Star Print-O-Bind, Okhla, New Delhi-20

PADMA PURANA
by : Dr. Vinay

Contents

A. Srishti Khanda   **11**
  1. Dialogue: Bhishma and Pulastya   11
  2. Lakshmi's Origin   13
  3. (a) Solar   14
    (b) Lunar Dynasty   16
  4. Brihaspati's Hoodwink   17
  5. Pushkar, the holy Teerth   18
  6. Saraswati becomes *Nanda*   19
  7. Worst Pain and Best Donation   20
  8. The Tale of Teerth Nag (Nag-Teerth)   22
  9. The Birth of Mahishasura   23
  10. Vishnu, as boar (incarnation) slays Hiranyaksha   26
  11. Slaying of Hiranyakashyapu   27

B. Bhoomi Khanda   **32**
  1. Dialogue: Soma Sharma and Vasishtha   33
  2. Vena's Story   36
  3. The Story of Yayati   41

C. Swarga Khanda   **44**

D. Brahma Khanda   **51**

E. Patal Khanda   **60**

F. Uttara Khanda   **72**
  1. Ekadashi Fast and Modes of Worship   80
  2. The Importance of Taking Bath   84
  3. Avatars of Lord Vishnu   87
  4. Srimad Bhagwadgita Cantos   97
  5. Raja Dilip and Nandini Cow   111
  6. Different Forms of Super Gods   113
  7. Kriya Yoga Saar (Essence of Human Actions)   114

Introduction

The Puranas are very important times for the Indian thought stream. They not only reveal the past history, ethos and values but also act as beacon to lighten man's future. These constitute an important source for revelation of seers, sages and great souls of yore. These explore the growth of Indian thoughts, which gradually shifted from the pure rituals of the Vedic era to pure metaphysics by the dawn of Upanishads.

Padma literally means a flower of lotus. *Padma Purana* discusses the origin of earth and the world as achieved by Brahma, the Creator. He was born in the form of *lotus* (He originated from the lotus emanating through the navel of lord Vishnu). The treatise had been appropriately titled *Padma-Purana*. Among the *Puranas* edited and reviewed by sage Vedavyas, it occupies the second place from the importance and the number of quatrains.

Vedavyas had laid down a criterion for any tome sing a *Purana*. It must have five characteristics: creation (of the world), its dissolution, dynastics that had ruled over it, the details of the Manu (who reigned supreme in each *Manvantara* or the Manu's era) and the details of royal dynasties (Vamsanucarita). In Sanskrit lingo, these are, *Sarga, Pratisarga, Vamsa, Manvantara* and *Vamsanucarita*. The *Padma-Purana* fulfills the aforementioned conditions. On being devoted to lord Vishnu's worship, it is called *Vaishnava Purana*. The modes of lord Vishnu's worship have been explained through episodes, stories and anecdotes better than they would have in other *Puranas*.

The *Padma Purana* has five parts (topics). The first part, i.e. *Shrishti-Khanda* tells how Brahma was born from the Padma (lotus). It then explains creation as per Samkhya terminology. Brahma, however, is being given prominence, absent in other *Puranas*. It extols the supremacy of lord Vishnu. It speaks of Prajapatis (Progenitors), Rudras (the dreadful formof lord Shiva), and Manus after treating the dimensions of time from an instant to the life span of Brahma. It states the importance of *Shraddhas*, especially at Gaya. It highlights about the lunar dynasty more elaborately than the solar. This part dwells upon observing *vratas* (fasts) at length. The subsequent part *Bhoomi-Khanda* explores the lives of *Prahlada* and *Vrittasura* besides *Vena* and *Prithvi*. It proceeds to enumerate the human embodiments of holiness (*Jangam Tirthas* i.e., the parents and the gurus) and the sacred shrines (*Sthavara Tirthas*) or the holy pilgrimage spots at Mahakata, Prabhasa, Kurukshetra. The third part or *Swarga-khanda* describes the upper strata inhabited by gods, in the course of king Bharat's ascension to Vaikuntha (abode of lord Vishnu) beyond *Dhruva-Mandala* (the realms of the Pole Star). It describes the four *Varnas* (castes) and the four *Ashramas* (phases of life) with earmarked duties, as well as *Karma-yoga* and *Gyaan Yoga*. The fourth part or the *Patala-khanda* (the nether realms) speaks of those realms below planet earth. It narrates in detail the exploits of the kings of the solar dynasty. *Bhagawata* is being extolled in this part as the last and the best of the *Puranas*.

The last part of *Padma-khanda* is the *Uttara-khanda*, which deals with the story of the demon king *Jalandhara*. It applauds the *mantras* (hymn) *Om Lakshmi Narainaabhyaam Namah* as the splendid mantra and asserts that it could be imparted to all varnas including the *shoodras* and women after diksha (initiation). It describes the *Para*, *Vyooha* and *Vibhava* aspects of lord Vishnu, and emphasizes on the sanctity of the month of *Kaartika*. It discusses *Kriya-yoga*, dealing with practical devotion, distinct from *Dhyana-Yoga* or the royal path of contemplation.

The *Puranas* like the Padma Purana, form the basic text of the Indian mass on social, cultural, religious and political spheres. The texts play important role in shaping life and culture among the Indians and describe pre-set pattern of social, monetary, geographical, political, philosophical religious and educational systems. The *Puranas* have presented similar synthesism in cosmology and lead the *Pauranikas* (the authors of *Puranas*) to find a link among various things, creatures, creeds, thoughts, sects and systems through their witty myths. The apparent garb of myths may look rather absurd as the prima facie viewing but the real essence within remains quite enlightening and educative. Integration of different cultural stands, thoughts, traditions and giving dynamics to the society, the bigger role is being played by any society of the world history and literature as that of *Puranas*. The relevance lies therein during any time as in the modern times, as well.

Some of the stories have been dramatized deliberately in order to make the narration more interesting. The emphasis on the present work reveals great thought process of the Indian mind to the uninitiated and the x-generation to make them realize what India was. The author or the compiler of the Purana, remains very grateful to Mr. Narendra Kumar of Diamond Pocket Books for extending support to prepare this treatise.

May the tribe increase.

B.K. Chaturvedi

A. Srishti - Khanda

1. Dialogue: Bhishma and Pulastya

[Bhishma, the grand sire of the *Mahabharat* was an erudite par excellence apart from being a fearless archer. *Padma Purana* opens with dialogue between *Bhishma* and the sage *Pulastya*, the grand sire of Ravana (*Ramayana*). Is not it a sheer coincidence? This is how sage Vedavyas had applauded *Padma Purana*.]

Bhishma inquired Pulastya: "Oh Great sage! Tell me something about the creation of world. How the desire to create engineered with Brahma, the Creator's heart?

Pulastya replied: 'Oh great Kshatriya! Brahma is eternal and so will be his actions. It was on the direction of lord Supreme that He conceived of creating the world for the sustenance of species. There can be no time frame about His actions. For, His time-frame[1] is totally different from that of we, the human beings.'

Explaining the difference between the two time-frames, the sage told Bhishma, 'A human day and night is made of 60 *ghatis*. Each *paksha* (24 *pakshas* in a human-year) has 15 such day-night units. A month has two fortnights. Six

---

1. The existence of two time fames is absolutely a moral concept unfound in any civilization or culture of the entire world except the Indian. Curiously enough the same idea was proved by the famous mathematician and scientist, Albert Einstein only in the beginning of the 20th century which fetched him the covetous Nobel Prize. He proved that Time was not constant and universal measures will alter when some object travels with the velocity of light, a constant. This concept is available in the Indian ancient tomes with a few stories woven around the theme.

months make an *ayana*. One year contains two *ayanas*. These *ayanas* are called *Uttarayana* (when the sun moves northward vis-a-vis planet earth) and *Dakshinayana* (when the sun moves southward vis-a-vis planet earth). A lunar year is equal to one day of gods (called the divine year). This kind of thousands of years make a cycle of the *Satya, Treta, Dwapara* and *Kali* yuga. One full cycle of these four ages make one day of Brahma.

During one day of Brahma, there reigns 14 Manus by counting this way, Brahma is only just a year old.

Having known about the human and the divine time divisions, Bhishma desired to know about the process of creation of the world. Pulastya weaved over the details.

In the beginning, there was nothing but darkness. The earth lay sunken under water. Brahma realized the position and approached lord Vishnu for succour. Lord Vishnu assumed the form of a boar and retrieved planet earth from the abyss. Lord Vishnu sought Brahma to start the process of creation afresh. The creation incorporated basic qualities--Sattva, Raja and Tama.* Pulastya told Bhishma that *Sattva Guna* characteristics emerged from Brahma's mouth, *Rajo Guna* characteristics from His breast and thighs while *Tamo Guna* characteristics surfaced through His feet. These organs of Brahma became the founts of creation of classes-*Brahmana, Kshatriya, Vaishya and Shoodra.*

Brahma assorted His creation into four categories. Each of them is being vested with basic duty. Conducting Yajna became the bounden duty of Brahmanas. It accounted for the virtues and extent of happiness during one's survival. He created various realms for the dwelling of the Brahmanas, Kshatriyas, Vaishyas and Shoodras, as well. He accommodated Prajapati, Indra, Gandharvas and other sub-divine species and the demons, accordingly. He created heaven for the virtuous to enjoy comforts and hell for punishing the wretched.

Having done the major work of creation, Brahma created nine psychic sons for His support. They are Bhrigu, Pulastya, Pulaha, Ritu, Angira, Mareechi, Daksha, Atri and Vasishtha. The nine psychic sons are called *Bramhatma Vai Jayate Putrah*. His earlier sons, viz., Sanaka, Sanandana, Sanatana and Sanat Kumar evinced no interest in furthering creation. Angered by these four *child-sons*, indifference over a brilliant beam of radiation emerged from His forehead, creating Ardhanarishwara (a behemoth with half male and half female appearance) or Rudra. Individual Man and Woman owe to Rudra. Brahma called the two primal existence in the human form as Swayambhu Manu and Shatarupa, who were the prime progenitors of the human race (homo sapiens). The pair gave birth to four issues: Priyavrata, Uttanapada, Prasuti and Aakuti. Aakuti was married to Ruchi and Prasuti to Daksha. Daksha and Prasuti gave birth to 24 daughters, married to various sages. Among those 13 were married to Dharmaraja, Bhrigu was married to Khyati, Bhava (Shiv) to Sati, Marichi to Sambhuti, Angira to Smriti, Pulastya to Preeti, Pulaha to Kshama, Kriti to Sannati, Atri to Anusooya, Vasishtha to Arundhati (also called Urja), Vahva to Swaah and the Pitri to Swadha. The entire human race of creation owes to them.

Bhishma sought Pulastya about the origin of Lakshmi, the goddess of all virtues and glory. The sage reciprocated with due regards.

2. Lakshmi's Origin

Once wandering across the earth, the furious sage Durvasa happened to find beautiful garland. It looked divine and remain resplendant. He realized the extent of uncontrollable libido on wearing around his neck. He found quite peeved at the development, which made him approach Indra. He entered the heaven and gave the garland to Indra.

Indra put that garland round his favourite mount Eiravat's (elephant's) neck, who casually threw it down the earth. Durvasa, who lost his temperament at the dishonour by Indra, cursed him to be deprived of resplendance and opulence. Although Indra beg forgiveness for the error, Durvasa iterated that curse could not be taken back. Soon Indra and his fellow-gods were expelled from heaven by the mighty demons.

Indra felt rather miserable and sought Brahma's help. Brahma took him to lord Vishnu, who advised Indra to compromise with demons and arrange an yajna. The yajna involved churning of ocean to retrieve the lost glory of heaven and goddess Lakshmi. Lord Vishnu embraced the form of an enchantress (Mohini), to deprive the demons swallow the nectar, given to gods. The gods thereby recaptured heaven with goddess Lakshmi. Lakshmi choose to marry lord Vishnu with whom she remains forever.

Pulastya continued about Lakshmi's antecedents, told that Lakshmi was born as a daughter to sage Bhrigu and his wife Khyati. Lakshmi during her unmarried state, created a full city (*pur*) which she sought her father to guard. She anticipated to get back after her marriage. Bhrigu refused. This led to a feud between Bhrigu and lord Vishnu. Bhrigu cursed lord Vishnu that he should get separated from his consort during Treta era. The curse worked out with lord Ram swerved from His consort Sita, often.

3. (a) Solar Dynasty

Pulastya, on being asked by Bhishma about the antecedents of Solar Dynasty told him about the details.

Vaivasvata Manu had the sons: Ila, Ikshvaaku, Kushnaam, Arishta, Dhrishta, Narishyanta, Karush, Mahabali, Sharyati and Prashadha. Vaivasvata Manu coronated eldest son Ila and left for the wild. Ila, for getting more riches moved out to defeat enemies. He managed to defeat many opponents. He entered the prohibited boulevarde of lord Shankar on the foothills of Himalaya. That area was earmarked for lord Shankar and spouse Parvati's to have fun without the entry of any male person. As Ila entered the prohibited zone, not only he but his solders become transexual, or women instantly. It was in that form, Ila begot a boy for the earthy ruler Pururava, who became known as Budha (planet Mercury). Owing to king Ila, changing his sex, the entire prohibited region became known as *Ila vritta*. Ila had three mighty sons· Utkala, Gayae and Haritaashwa. The other sons of Vaivasvata Manu too have their progeny. Nashiyanta had Shukra, Naabhag-Ambarisha, Dhrishta-Dhristaketu, Swadharm- Ranadhrishta, Sharyati-Aanarta and daughter Sukanya. Aanarta had an industrious son Rochiman. He called the entire region as Aanarta and begot Reva from the wife Kushasthali. Revati, the grand daughter of Rev got doubled with Balram, the elder brother of lord Krishna.

Manu's second son Ikshavaaku begot sons Vikukshi, Nimi and Dandak. The dynasty had personalities like king Harishchandra, Rohitashva - Vrisha, Bahu and Sagar. Sagar had two wives Prabhavati and Bhanumati. Prabha begot some 60,000 sons while Bhanumati begot son Asmanjasa. It was Asmanjasa's dynasty that ultimately had Bhagirath who made the celestial river Ganges (Ganga) descend planet earth to glorify some 60,000 souls of grand uncles. The saga of Solar dynasty is endless giving birth to several mighty kings.

The Manes: The Pitris (Manes) are seven in heaven. The four of them are Moortika, while the three are Amoortika. Their habitat is believed to be deep south. The Manes must be revered by descendants through rituals (Shraddha) and other related ceremonies after their demise.

There are three kinds of Shraddha: Nitya, Naimittika and Kaamya. On the day of Shraddha, some well read and noble Brahmin should be fed and gift a cow and land, as dakshina. The important days for Shraddha are the second (lunar) day of the month Ashwini, ninth (lunar) day of Kartika (bright half), tenth (lunar) day of Aashadh, and eighth (lunar) day of Shravan. The Shraddha performed across the holy pilgrimage spots (teerth) bring special merit to the descendent.

(b) Lunar Dynasty

Chandra or the Moon is believed to be the prime progenitor of the dynasty. Atri sat under penance for sufficient long period on the insistence of his father Brahma to multiply human population of the world. His immobility with wide opened eyes welled up water which made directions withdrew from space. The latter produced a brilliant boy called Chandrama (the Moon). Chandra underwent deep penance to appease lord Vishnu for glorification. He became one of the gods and was empowered to receive due share of yajna performed by seers and beings. His arrogance made him to elope with the divine preceptor Brihaspati's wife Tara. Although Chandra released Tara at the insistence of superior gods, but not before making her pregnant. Tara, eventually begot Budh (planet Mercury), heralded as the son of Brihaspati, but took birth on the physical union of Chandra with Tara. Budh had produced with the union of female Ila (as told before) Pururava. Pururava had eight issues with his union from the celestial danseuse, Urvasi. Aayu was their most industrious sons, who begot five sons. The most prominent among them was Raji, who was proud of fathering 100 sons, known as Rajesh. Raji had propitiated lord Vishnu to triumph over gods and demons, alike. The gods took Raji's support to vanquish demons. Raji adopted Indra and bequeathed his kingdom and left for the jungle. However, Raji's sons usurped Indra's kingdom. Indra complained to preceptor Brihaspati, who cursed them of apostasy. Subsequently, Indra managed to kill the sons of Raji with the connivance of the preceptor Brihaspati.

Aayu's first son Nahush had seven sons called Yati, Yayati, Sharyati, Uttara, Para, Ayati and Niryati. Yayati, among them became the king who begot Druhya, Anu and Puru from first wife and Yadu as well as Turvashu from second wife Devayani.

Pulastya narrated later of an anecdote of how Brahaspati attempted to hoodwink demons galore.

4. Brihaspati's Hoodwink

A fierce battle ensued once between the gods and the demons vanquished demons. Shukracharya, the preceptor of demons was appalled. He decided to undergo rigorous penance to empower demons. Indra learnt about the intention of preceptor of demons, he sent his daughter Jayanti to seduce Shukracharya. Jayanti looked after him well, but Shukracharya managed to receive blessings from lord Shiva. Having completed the mission Shukracharya choose to enjoy 100 year-company with Jayanti, who had influenced him appreciably by her charms.

Preceptor Brihaspati acquired details from Indra and learnt Shukracharya's absence from his position for about 100 years. He approached demons in the guise of Shukracharya and wean themselves from divine pursuits. He managed to tell the demons that they should perform Yajnas. The demons failed to detect Brahaspati's real identity and blindly followed his advise. Meanwhile, the period of 100 years elapsed and Shukracharya returned to know about the celestial preceptor practising. Shukracharya tries to impress upon his disciples that their present preceptor was an impersonator, but they didn't believe him. On the other hand, they told the real preceptor about the advantages of doing yajna. Whereupon Shukracharya questioned: 'If by being sacrificed at the altar of the yajna the animal gets heaven, then why don't the protagonists of yajna sacrifice their father similarly?' Shukracharya brought the demons back to the original path. Arhant, a stranger taught the demons to abandon the demonic path. Arhant asked them to shave off their heads, remain ever naked or unclad like a mendicant or 'Bhikshu'. The demons began to dwell like the medicants on the banks of the river Narmada.

Brihaspati was quite happy with the success of his mission of weaning the demons away from Shukracharya's fold. Now when Indra, having learnt the details from Brihaspati, reached before the demons in the guise of hermit and told Indra, 'O celestial king reigning over heavens, we have quit the demonic path'. Indra was delighted to find the demons to have turned over a new leaf. Shukracharya again made the demons as they were cruel and revolt against the gods, shedding artificial behaviour caused by the influence of Brihaspati and Arhant.

5. Pushkar, the holy Teerth

Brahma thought at his abode, 'Though I am the creator, I have no place on the earth known by my name. I must find a place glorified in my name.' He took a lotus in hand and traversed the entire earth. There was one place on earth where that flower slipped suddenly from hand. The place where that flower fell developed into a huge pond with severe impact. That place became known as Pushkar, which literally in Sankrit, means a pond. He performed yajna there, in which sage Brigu was the organizer (Hota) and Pulastya (the narrator became the clergy reading Sama Vedic hymns) (Adhvaryu). However, the yajna needed to be performed with the spouse. Although, Brahma's wife, Savitri, was called she refused to come. Since the auspicious time was getting elapsed, Brahma asked Indra to arrange for him an additional wife. Indra went out and kidnapped a beautiful girl selling curds and milk. She was given the name Gayatri. But by the time, Savitri managed to reach there, she was shocked to find Brahma performing yajna with another wife. Although, she was duly pacified by Vishnu's efforts, Savitri couldn't help herself and cursed Gayatri, 'You shall never be worshipped except Kartik Purnima.'

After completion of the yajna, the residue of the amber was put into the sea from which emerged a subterranean stream called Saraswati. It was this river that used to flow in Pushkar. She was subsequently called Nanda. Pulastya recalled the anecdote relating to this episode before Bhishma.

6. Saraswati becomes *Nanda*

King Prabhanjan reigned near the pilgrimage spot Kurukshetra some time ago. Once he was on a hunting spree and happened to shoot his arrow at a doe, feeding her baby. The doe cursed the king to become a demon. The king pleaded for his ignorance, whereupon the doe assured the curse would end up, provided the king traverses many species till he meet the cow by name Sunanda.

It happened so that after having taken rebirth among many species the king entered the tiger species. Often, he spotted a very beautiful cow and was about to devour her, when the cow bemoaned, 'Wait, till I feed my child. You can then merrily devour me.' The cow appeared before the tiger after milching her calf, the beast was impressed by her honesty. The tiger, who was actually king Prabhajan in a tiger's species decided not to eat her. The curse ended as he beheld the cow. King Prabhanjan cried, 'O cow Sunanda! I had tested your honesty on the orders of Dharmaraj. You can have your share of boon, since you have proved your honesty. The cow besought to become river Saramati in

Pushkar lake. That is why River Saraswati is known as Nanda flowing across Pushkar. Else, it is known as Saraswati. In Pushkar, the cow Sunanda gets her name to have her glory ever indicated [Now that mysterious river Saraswati remains extinct in not only Pushkar, but all over India]

River Saraswati oozes from Ganga's arrival on Earth

Recollecting the saga of the holy Teerth Pushkar, Pulastya told Bhishm that it was in Pushkar that Indra had received the sturdy bones of sage Dadheechi to kill the demon Vrittasur. Twastha converted bones into the thunderbolt for Indra. Since Vrittasur was Brahman, Indra had to suffer the consequences of a 'brahmicide'. (murdering a brahman). Out of fear on account of carrying this charge, Indra had to hid inside a pond. The gods were expelled from heaven on the prayers of Indra . Lord Vishnu conveyed the message to Indra that he should go to the bank of Saraswati river where sage Agastya was under meditation. 'If the sage drinks up the ocean you (god) may reach upto Indra soon.' The gods reached Pushkar lake and prayed Agastya to help their predicament. Agastya agreed to drank the ocean up for the welfare of gods and people. Eventually, Indra was absolved of the charges of killing a Brahmin.

The situation turned into another development. The ocean went dry on being sapped out of water. It was dug out but in vain. Brahma reassured the gods the ocean would remain filled forever on the arrival of Ganga to earth from heaven.

7. Worst Pain and Best Donation

Pulastya continued to recollect severe drought on earth, to Bhishma. Not only the hearts and common men, but even the sages like Atri and Vasishtha were to suffer from the predicament. Although the kings donated the sages some edibles which they refused and reached the lotus pond of Pushkar. An ascetic Shunah-Shepa camped on its banks. Atri and Vasishtha inquired the ascetic, 'What is the worst pain?' The ascetic replied: 'That which is caused by the pangs of hunger. A hungry man has no scruples. He can do the most forbidden things driven by his hunger.' The sages inquired again, 'What is the best alms for donation?' 'Cereals and edible things. Only that can satiate hungry.' And what is the best Tapa (penance)?' Suppressing one's desires and cravings which can really make a man lord over his destiny. Yajnas and Vratas are of no use, if they don't suppress one's natural desires. He who regards women as adorable as his own mother and other's riches no better than the clode of earth goes beyond the travails of this desires and attains Salvation in the real sheen.'

Focusing upon the glories of the holy Pushkar Tertha, Pulastya told Bhishm that 'He who performs the Vrata of Dwadashi of the Magh lunar month gets happiness from his wife and kids. Many kings like Pushpavahan and Dharmamurti could get all comforts and happiness by performing these Vratas at Pushkar.

Pulastya told Bhishma: 'Once in Satya Yuga, the demons managed to defeat gods and established their laws across the universe. The creator Brahma often told that demons had become so powerful owing to the boon they have received, when the gods sought his grace. Lord Vishnu alone could mesmerize those demons.'

Pulastya continued, 'Then on Brahma's request, lord Vishnu decided to appear as a small boy-Vaman to brow beat demons. Later, a 16-year old boy reached before the demon lord Bali when the latter completed an yajna and was about to dole out alms to brahmins congregated. Vaman joined the queue of those brahmins. Shukracharya, the preceptor of demons had recognized lord Vishnu and warned Bali to remain wary of His mischievous designs.

But that brave king said: If lord Vishnu comes before me as medicant, I shall be happy to donate whatever he demands.'

Vaman demanded three steps of the land and Bali agreed. Soon Vaman became as high as to touch even the sky. In first such step, he covered the entire earth, and in the subsequent step towards the heaven. Brahma immediately recognized when his one foot reached heaven and washed lord's foot with obeisance through water from his kamandal. That stream of water with which Vaman's (or Vishnu's) foot was washed became the river that filled the pond of Pushkar. 'That is why, it is so holy,' concluded Pulastya [This story is also recounted for the birth of the Ganga river in other Puranas].

Bhishma inquired: 'Sage! Where did Lord Vishnu as Vaman had put his last step?' On the head of Bali which just pressed him down to the nether world (Patal). Since then Bali rules only over Patal.

8. The Tale of Teerth Nag (Nag-Teerth)

'Many deadly snakes, like Takshaka, Vasuki, Mahabal, Karkotaka, Nagendra. Kulika and Shankh were inhabiting the universe during the olden days. Human race was virtually subjected to insecurity . Creator Brahma was quite worried and admonish the species. He predicted their days of survival are nearer in Dwapar Yuga. However, the snake Brahma did was in accordance with the nature's laws imparted by Brahma. In case of anything wrong done by the species, He must set limits for their movement.' Brahma allowed the species to survive in Sutala (plains) Vitala (shallow land) and Taalatala (underground) and sting only the wicked and rogues. Brahma assured him and his race from extinction through his sister Jaratkaru, during the yajnas by Janmejaya of Pandavas, Brahma made them stay near the unbroken stream with faces northwards. That place is now famous as Nag-Teertha', replied Pulastya.

Continuing with the saga, Pulastya said that Pushkar was famous place, where one's prayer reunites with one's brethren. This was iterated by sage Atri when lord Ram sought the place to end estrangement from brethren. Lord Rama reached the spot during banishment and performed obsequies for departed relatives and manes.

9. The Birth of Mahishasura

Once a naughty girl frightened a sage by farting from her mouth besides bellowing like a buffalo. The sage on being peeved cursed her to stay as buffalo for one hundred years. The girl apologized and sought redemption for which the sage assured: 'the day you beget son resembling a buffalow from your womb, you will be revert to human form.

The girl happened to bathe in a river nearby after couple of days. She decided to bathe unclad on seeing the place totally desolate. She immersed herself deep water when a valiant king Sindhudweep was on errands. He got his semen ejaculated on noticing the unclad voluptious female in the sea. Unknowingly that girl, called Mahishi, happened to drink the water containing his semen which made her conceive and beget a behemoth. The boy resembled a buffalo by features, and was known as Mahishasura. He become lecherous as he grew up. Once Narad came to his court and told Mahishasura about an incompatible beauty named Khemankari. Mahishasura immediately sent his courier with the proposal and details about Mahishasura - a scion of reputed linage and the son of brilliant king Sindhudweep. The queen Khemankari laughed with contempt and responded as 'let alone our queen even the maids won't accept that buffalo-man as husband'. This provoked the courier enough to fight in an unavoidable war. The ensuing war brought sage Narada on the scene, who warned the queen about Mahishasura defeating gods but his undaunted spirit made her spinisters reciprocate with courage. The queen killed Mahishasura by invoking the grace of lord Rudra in the dual.

The gods were delighted at the relief from the onslaughts of the demon. They established a temple of mata Khemankari and applauded her feat and returned to their realms.

Concluding the story Pulastya said that the demon Mahishasura symbolized evil while Mata Khemankari the embodiment of knowledge. Only knowledge can submerge ignorance and whenever it envelop human mind, the god's succour brings saviour to protect the rule of law and norms of perpetuity.

The Four Yugas

Upon Bhishma's query, sage Pulastya continued on the characteristics of each of the four aeons that form one cycle of time. In Satya Yuga, the righteousness was four legs, in Treta upon three legs, in Dwapara upon two legs and in Kaliyuga only upon one leg. Kaliyuga ends in sole inequity with reigning over of unrighteousness. This rule of impropriety subjects Mother nature under upheaval so much that it would fold up on the Doom's day, to commence the cycle afresh. Each age has its measure in the divine years: Satya Yuga - 4,000 years; Treta Yuga - 3,000 years, Dwapara Yuga 2,000 years, while Kaliyuga of 1,200 years. At the end of one cycle of Ages, God withdraws the creation by making all fiery elements accumulate as fire; watery as water, earthy as solid earth, and airy as the sky. Finally, everything vanishes and the lord Almighty think: 'Ekoham Bahusyamaha' and creation again comes into existence.

Kartikeya's Story

When Bhishma expressed the desire of knowing about Kartikeya's birth, Pulastya obliged.

At the very beginning of creation, by the venture of the prime couple: Kashyapa and Diti, having received a boon, had a powerful son called, Vajranga. At his mother bidding, he brought Indra tied fully at his mother's feet and began contemplating to slay the divine chief. Kashyapa and Brahma have impressed upon Vajranga that Indra, being the celestial chief shouldn't be killed. Vajranga released Indra. One day, Vajranga went to the woods after his marriage. Indra came in his absence and tortured Vajranga's lovely wife quite severely. When Vajranga learnt about Indra's mischief on his return, he asked his wife to bear it patiently as the time was not ripe for retaliation with Indra. After sometime, Vajranga's wife gave birth to a robust son. He was so powerful that demon kings made him their overlord. He was named Tarakasura. In order to have total command over his enemies - the gods, Tarakasura went to the Himalayas to propitiate Brahma and win from him the boon of invincibility and immortality. Brahma duly appeared and said: 'You are a mortal being, so you must die one day. I cannot make you invincible, either as that needs to be won by one's self efforts. You may have some other boon.' Tarakasura said: 'Ensure that I should never be killed by anybody else to save a seven year old boy.' Brahma said: 'So be it' and quickly disappeared.

Getting this boon, the demon lord Taraka collected troops of robust demons and attacked the god's realm. They defeated the divine forces. The survivors fled for safety. Tarakasura ordered troops that no god should be killed, but be arrested. When his trusted lieutenant, Kalanemi did so, Taraka released his enemies except Indra. He shaved off Indra's head, got his body marked by dog's feet and ordered demons release him after donning in whilt robes. Thus severely dishonoured Indra returned to his realm.

The gods were severely nervous. They sought Brahma's help. Brahma told them: 'Wait for some more time. Only Shankar's son could kill him. Make Shankar agree for marriage The girl for him has already taken birth in the mountain chief's house. [He then narrates the entire tales of lord Shankara's marriage to Parvati and the burning of Kama Deva etc.]

After Shiv's marriage to Parvati, the gods began to wait for lord Shankara's siring a son. Gods sent Agni (the fire god) to find out the cause when much time elapsed without anything happened. Shankar was copulating with Parvati, when Agni reached Kailash. Seeing Agni, he disengaged himself from his wife's body. In this process, he had ejaculation, but his seed was gathered by Agni and put it into a pond. It was so hot that even Agni couldn't hold it. As it happened, Parvati happened to drink water from that pond which eventually made her pregnant. Parvati, at last gave birth to a six-faced son. He was named Kartikeya, as he grew up a little, he was made the divine force commandant. The gods attached Tarakasura and Kartikeya managed to kill Taraka with the help of his father Shiva. [This story is quite at variance with the standard story of Kartikeya's birth found in other Puranas].

10. Vishnu, as boar (incarnation) slays Hiranyaksha

Kashyapa and Diti had two sons, named Hiranyaksha and Hiranyakashyapa. The two brothers were, in the previous birth, the door-keepers of Vishnu's abode Varikuntha. Once they tried to stop Sanat-Kumar and his brother from entering the realm. Enraged the child-saints cursed them to become deadly demons in their successive three births. The door-keepers, named Jaya and Vijaya were reborn as Hirankyaksha and Hiranyakashyapu in their next birth.

Hiranyaksha was so powerful that he controlled all realms. In order to capture the gods' realm, he performed a most rigid penance to propitiate Brahma. Although, Brahma denied him the boon of invincibility, he granted much power to control the realms.

As he returned from the Himalayas, he become so arrogant that he took the earth down to the abyss. This disturbed the entire emotion. He also defected the ruler of water, Varuna. Thus, he became the king of the heaven, the earth and the underworld. When he took the earth down to the abyss of the ocean, the gods prayed lord Vishnu, who appeared as behemoth boar to retrieve the earth to its normal level and defeated Hiranyaksha.

The same way at the gods, request demon Madhu was killed by lord Vishnu. Since then lord Vishnu earned another epithet as 'Madhava' meaning the slayer of the demon Madhu. [These Asuras had invariably received the boon only from Brahma or Shiva and never from Vishnu who always came in different form to slay such demons. It is because Vishnu's job is preservation of the rule of law on this earth and hence getting rid of those that disturb the righteous rule.]

11. Slaying of Hiranyakashyapu

Hiranyaksha's brother Hiranyakashyapu was furious when he learn Vishnu slaying Hiranyaksha in the form of a boar. In order to teach Vishnu a bitter lesson, Hiranyakashyapu went for performing severe penance to gain much power from Brahma. He duly propitiated Brahma who granted him the boon that he could never be killed by night or day, by man or beast; in the sky or on the earth, by any weapon, neither inside a house nor out of it. Thus guarded against death in all possible way, Hiranyakashyapu became much powerful and he began to rub over the entire universe, defying the gods domain who were also thrown out of their realms.

But no matter what precautions Hiranyakashyapu had taken, be had a rebel in his own family. By quirk of the divine scheme, his son Prahlad became an arch devote of lord Vishnu. The father tried his level best to persuade son but that did not work. Then enraged father tried to murder his son through a variety of means. But each time Vishnu secretly intervened to save Prahlad.

Meanwhile, driven out of heaven, the gods were in great trouble. They had been deprived of their shares in yajna by the demon-lord, Hiranyakashapu. In disperation, they went and prayed lord Vishnu, who promised them a solution to their problem.

One day Hiranyakashyapu called Prahlad and said: 'How is it that you escaped each time when at my orders my men tried to kill you.'

'Because lord Vishnu saved me,' replied Prahlad. 'My Lord Vishnu is everywhere.'

'What do you mean everywhere?' retorted Hiranyakashyapu. He pointed to a crystal pillar inside the palace and asked: 'Is Vishnu inside the pillar as well?'

'Yes' replied Prahlad.

'Very well then, I am going to break this pillar in twain.' As he raised his mace and hit with the pillar, there arose a deafening sound. The pillar burst forth into pieces and out emerged from it a peculiar figure----a giant with the head of a lion. He caught hold of Hiranyakashyapu and placed the demon across his thighs. And then with his claws that giant tore apart the demon's chest and killed Hiranyakashyapu instantly. Brahma's boon to Hiranyakashapu had been that the demon would not be killed by man or beast. But giant (Vishnu) was neither a man nor a beast. The boon had said that the demon would not be killed in the sky, the water or the earth. Nrisimha (that giant) eventually killed the demon on lord Vishnu (Nrisimha's) thighs which formed neither the earth nor the sky but a queer place--mid air.

Hiranyakashyapa was killed at the twilight zone, which was neither the day nor the night. And finally he was killed by Nrisimha at the threshold of the palace which was neither inside or outside of any building. Thus Brahma's boon had been scrupulously maintained by Vishnu and yet he managed to kill that demon lord.

After Hiranyakashyapu was killed, the gods were rightfully restored to heaven. Lord Vishnu made Prahlad the ruler of the Asuras. [It was Prahlad's grandson Bali, who faced lord Vishnu in the Vamana (dwarf) form. That story has been referred to already].

The Norms of Ideal Conduct

The progeny should give all respect and honour to their parents; the wife should ever be devoted to her husband against odds; having a sympathetic feeling for all beings of the world. In order to emphasise their norms, Pulastya told Bhishm the stories of Tuladhara, of the computation between Kartikeya and Ganesha (in which Ganesha circumambulated round his parents to win the race of early marriage and established the fact that the parents symbolized the entire would etc.).

In order to highlight the unique devotion, Pulastya recounted the story of Saivya. She was a devoted woman to her husband who was a lecher, but longed to have enjoyment with a prostitute. Since, her husband had become immobile due to the disease, the devoted wife herself agreed to take that lecherous person (her husband) to that prostitute. The night had fallen by that time and she took her husband on her back in the middle of the night - the time told by that prostitute to bring her husband. While moving amidst dark streets, she happened to pass very close to the sage Mandavya, who was meditating in absolute trance. That collision disturbed the sage's trance and he cursed that he whose body collided against his meditative body should die by the next day at sunrise. In fact, it has the hanging leg of that leper that had touched the sage's body. Now by that curse of the sage, Saivya's husband was sure to die at the sunrise, next morning. But Saivya, who had earned enough merit by her devoted services to her husband said: 'If I have ever been faithful to my husband may the sun not rise tomorrow.'

And it so happened that the next day the sun didn't appear, making the conditions of the world go haywire. People panicked. When the gods went to Brahma and made Brahma question the sun the reason for his not appearing at the scheduled time, the Sun-god said: 'I couldn't dare defy the orders of a Sati. (devoted wife)'. Meanwhile, sage Mandavya's prestige was also at stake, as his cure was not vindicated. At last Brahma asked the sun to appear and promised to Saivya: 'Your husband would die at the sunrise only bodily and not in existence. He, after his death, will immediately get a new and fair body.' This way the sage's curse and that of Saivya's prediction was reconciled. This episode highlighted the glory of a devoted wife to her husband even through he was a leper and a lecher as well. Pulastya further said that nothing was impossible for a holy devoted woman.

Talking about the meritorious deeds, Pulastya told Bhishma that building a pond, digging a well, arranging for quenching the thirst of the common people, growing shade-giving trees and building bridges across the rivers were some of the very meritorious deeds. Among planting trees, planting the trees of 'Amla' and planting the Tulsi plants were specially meant bestowing 'Vasudeva has special liking for the fruits of Amla, which tremendously adds to maintaining good health of people. Also the planting of Tulsi plants ensure the house remaining beyond the reach of ghosts and diseases. Even lord Ram and lord Krishna had done so. Among the merit accruing deeds taking bath in the river Ganga is rated very high. Ganga is veritably mother for the people caring for her.'

As far as modes of worship are concerned, Pulastya impressed upon Bhishma that worshipping God is the best mode is doing with feeling. But in all kinds of worship, the devotee must worship lord Ganesh first. Once Indra had tried to defy this rule and lost all his glory. Then on the advice of Brihaspati, he devotedly worshipped lord Ganesha to get back his lost kingdom and glory.

A person should leave his bed at least one and half hours before the sunrise and after getting through his morning cleansing rituals should worship God and then do the Sun-worship. Worshipping the sun specially on the 7th lunar day (Saptami) particularly on a Sunday with five red flowers grants the devotee much merit. If the transition of the Sun from one Zodiac sign to the other be taking place on Saptami and Sunday, it is the most auspicious mahurta for those who want their sins to be dissolved and merits to accumulates. While for the worship of the Sun, red-flowers (Java-Kusum) should be used, for the worship of Mother Goddess Durga, blue flowers should be employed. In fact, worshipping all the nine planets on their due days makes the devotee get over all his troubles.

Concluding his narration, Pulastya told Bhishma: 'O great scion of a noble family, in this section called Srishti Khanda, I told you about various merit bestowing deeds and the prominent incarnations of lord Vishnu.'

While recounting this dialogue, Sootaji, the narrator of all Puranas in the holy tirth of Naimisharanya before the huge assembly of noble saints and seers, said: 'Hearing this Srishti Khanda of the Padma Purana bestow the merits upon the listener as much as one gets after performing a hundred Ashwamedha Yajnas. He who reads or listens to these parts of Padma Purana ensure one's entering into the Supreme Abode of the lord Almighty following his quitting the mortal coil.

❏❏❏

B. Bhoomi Khanda

Beholding lord Vishnu's great curiosity in listening more about life on this planet and its growth and development Pulastya. continued his narration.

In the very beginning, there appeared sage Kashyapa, who had two wives Aditi and Diti. Aditi's sons were called the gods (or Aditya) and those from Diti were known as the demons(or Daityas). Both of them moved on diametrically opposite paths. Gods followed the path of propriety, morality and of Dharma, whereas the demons pursued that of sensual enjoyments, cruelty and terror. Hence their confrontation was a foregone conclusion. Although on the strength of their sheer diabolical powers, the demons often defeated gods, the latter managed to regain lost glory by lord Vishnu's grace. 'Lord Vishnu is the upholder of all that is righteous, noble and virtuous,' said Pulastya.

However, once the demons were massacred in a great number. Seeing her sons so cruelly massacred, Diti even thought of committing suicide. Then Kashyapa impressed upon her that all thatgot birth must face death. This is the inviolable rule of nature. One should never sorrow for the destruction of this mortal body. All mundane relations survive on flimsy relationship of the body. That body is feign and destined to decay is the universal law. What is the ultimate truth in this feign world is lord Supreme and His this portion which is called soul. It is the soul that is eternal and not the body encompasses it.

While trying to normalize the woe begone Diti

Kashyapa said that 'a body becomes live when soul enters in it. The soul or Atma has two of is trusted lieutenants called Dhyana (concentration) and Gyana, called knowledge. They keep on warning the body that all mundane lords are feign as they have nothing eternal in them. In fact, the universal soul or Paramatma in every bit of creation is one. The distinction between them emerges out of their physical appearance. In fact, the world has four kinds of beings:

(i) the plants, trees etc., that originate from the seeds sown on the earth.

(ii) the insects that get created from the filth like sweat and other refuse of the body – the various insects and worms etc.

(iii) the beings that emerge out of an egg

(iv) the beings that originate from their mother's womb.

The same way there are four kinds of eatable matter on the earth. Chooshya (to be sucked), khadya (to be chewed), Leh (semi-liquid from like curds) and Peya (the palatable)

It is by eating these that man gets strength and becomes capable of creating his progeny. The progeny has a set pattern of birth, development and growth and decay and death. Since this is a law ordained by lord the Almighty, all have to follow it. Your progeny also followed this law though their act were improper which made them lose their life. When Kashyapa explained universal law to his wife Diti, she became much normal and shed the idea of committing suicide.

1. Dialogue: Soma Sharma and Vasishtha

Soma Sharma was an issueless fellow. When he didn't get any progeny, he went to the woods and become an ascetic. In the woods, he happened to meet sage Vasishtha and sought the real form of righteousness (Dharma). Explaining it, Vasishta said that Dharma has the following eleven pillars.

(i) *Tapa* : Getting rid of lust and desires is known as Tapa.

(ii) *Satya* : Seeing all women (except one's wife) as one's mother and deeming all the riches of others as worthless is the basic form of Truth or Satya.

(iii) *Daan [Alms – Giving]* : Donating food-items to the hungry is best alms-giving or Daan.

(iv) *Kshama (Forgiveness)*: Nursing no ill-will for anybody and practising forgiveness for even your enemy is real Kshama. Have no vengeance for anyone.

(v) *Poojan (Adoration)* : Worshipping a harmed Brahmin and offering one's reverence to him is real poojan.

(vi) *Shaucha (Cleanliness)* : Cleansing one's body physically and mentally is real shaucha or cleanliness.

(vii) *Shanti (Peace)* : Having no ill-will for anyone and behaving with everybody under even respect.

(viii) *Asteya (Non-stealing)*: Coveting for no riches owned by others and feeling content with whatever one has.

(ix) *Ahimsa : (Non-violence)*: Causing no trouble for anyone and eschewing any path of violence.

(x) *Dama (Continence)*: Having total control over one's senses.

(xi) *Gurusewa*: Serving one's Guru, mentor or seniors with total devotion and loyalty.

Those who follow these principles in letter and spirit actually follow the real path of Dharma, which take them towards moksha or salvation.

Sage Vasishta then enlightened Soma Sharma that be who flouted these principles easily killed the Dharma, whose punishment was getting next birth in lowly species or families dwelling in abominable condition. 'That is why a being should never be indifferent to one's righteous Dharma which is symbolized by lord Vishnu himself. He who follows Dharma has the lord dwelling in his own heart. You yourself have graduated to the Brahminhood on account of your following the principles of Dharma. In fact, you were originally a Shoodra."

Then dwelling on Soma Sharma's earlier birth, the sage told that "once a very noble Brahmin had come to your house (in earlier life) seeking night-long shetter. You and your wife have treated that noble Brahmin very nicely. Hearing about the sanctity of keeping fast on the Ekadashi Day from that Brahmin, your wife and you have observed that fast and kept that Brahmin will looked after. It is on account of that fast and the noble company you became a Brahmin in this life as well. But even in that life, you had infatuation for your progeny, which has resulted in your remaining issueless in this life as well. Although, it is to destine in your this life that you should get a son, worship of Vishnu can even alter the course of destiny. So you should worship lord Vishnu."

Eventually with lord Vishnu's worship, Soma Sharma managed to propitiate lord Vishnu and get from the lord his desired boon as well. Concluding the story, Pulastya said: 'In this impermanent and feign world, only lord Vishnu is eternal. He, who performs his devoted worship gets not only rewards in this life, but even salvation.'

2. Vena's Story

Bhishma expressed then the desire of knowing about Raja Vena who was a very noble king. 'But what made him do something as to get killed by even the Rishis (sages) Pulastya said: 'I shall narrate you this story of Raja Vena as I have heard from the mouth of my Guru.'

In olden times, there was a very powerful and religious minded king whose name was Vena. One day while he was sitting in his court, there arrived a queer ascetic. He was totally naked having peacock's feather in his under arms and a broom in one hand and a broken coconut shell in the other, which served the purpose of being receptacle of receiving alms. The king chided him for coming to an open court unclad and asked the ascetic to give his introduction.

'O king! I am the essence of all religious personified. Arhant is the god of faith that I preach and only kindness is the essence of faith. In my faith, there is no room for tapa, sandhya, offering oblations to the departed soul or performing yajna. Neither sacrifice of any being has any place in my faith. My faith stands on the premises that human body is created by various permutation and combinations of the five elements like a fish's movement creates bubbles in the ocean, similarly the five elements movement create beings in this world. Our belief is that combination of five elements gives life and their disparity yields death. Since life and death are the part of physical process, there is no sense in doing any obsequies rites or performing any birthday. There is nothing that is spiritual. Unlike your Sanatan faith, we don't accept that offering oblutions to Brahmin would ensure your departed ancestors getting it. Has anyone seen the state post death? How could your feeding a person will quench the thirst of a person sitting far away, let alone your ancestors getting any morsel of the food offered on the earth. This is all sheer bumkum.

If by sacrificing an animal you seek prosperity and happiness, may be sacrificing your near and dear may give you much better property, riches etc.'

That ascetic spoke so forcefully that Raja Vena became convinced of the superiority of his religion and decided to embrace it, leaving Sanatana Dharma. Although Vena's father tried to dissuade him, instead of heading to his father's advice, he began to heap insults on his sire and assenting that the ascetic's faith was the perennial faith or Sanatana Dharmas. When he spoke much against Vedic Dharma and did not listen to what the high sages have said, they chased him to drive him away from the capital. Fearing their on slaught Vena tool shelter inside a termite hill. The high sages eventually killed him.

But since Vena had died issueless, the sages churned his one to produces a child who was made the ruler of Mlechcha race. When they churned the other arm, they produced another child called Prithu, who proved to be a very noble king and the true devotee of lord Vishnu.

At this juncture Bhishma asked Pulastya that how could a noble king like Vena could be weaned away by an ascetic from this perennical faith. 'Is there something beyond one's thinking a deeds which makes one's destiny?'

Pulastya said: 'What makes one's destiny is the deed one does in the previous life? These deeds could be yours as well as your perents. Vena could leave his faith not because of his deeds, but owing to his mother Suneeti's one misdeed which made her receive a curse from a gandharva. The story is like this.' Sage Pulastya then narrated the following story.

Sunita was the daughter of the death-god (Mrtyu). She was very naughty and always relished disturbing those engrossed in meditation. Once, she happened to disturb the musical devotion of a gandharva, who on a quiet hill was practicing his music lessons. He cursed Suneeta that she would get a son who would eventually prove very wicked and that he would be killed by the high sages. When Sunita told her father, he said that she would have to suffer the cousequences of her misdeeds.

Meanwhile, there was a very learned son of a noble Brahmin, Atri. His name was Ang. One day, by dint of his penance and devotion, he could witness all the riches and luxuries enjoyed by the divine chief Indra. Returning home he asked his father: 'Certainly, provided you worship lord Vishnu with great devotion and seek a boon from him.'

Getting this guidance Atri went to the woods and performed a very rigorous penance. He did it with such feelings that lord Vishnu appeared before him. Ang requested the lord to grant him such son as could outrival Indra.' Lord said: 'Find a suitable wife for yourself and soon your wish will be fulfilled.'

Wow, it was a difficult proposition for Ang to find a bride for himself, as he had no contact with outside world. But on the suggestion of the divine danseuse (Apsaras) Rambha and Menaka, Sunita agreed to marry Ang. Eventually, Ang and Suneeta were married. But owing to the curse she received from a gandharva, she had to produce a son who would eventually become very wicked. And Ang's boon was that he was to get a son, who would outrival even Indra. So they had Vena as the son, who initially proved a very noble king and verily the Indra of the earth, but ultimately became a wicked person to vindicate the curse that Suneeta had received.'

The Tale of Devoted wife Shukala

Long long ago, there lied a noble brahma called Krikala in the city of Kashi. His wife was a very devoted lady named Shukala. One day, Krikala decided to go on pilgrimage Shukala requested Krikala to accompany her as well, but the latter refused on the plea that pilgrimage may involve much hardship which Shukala might not be able to bear. Although Shukala pleaded in a variety of ways, Krikala left alone for the pilgrimage, leaving his wife alone.

Now Shukala was much woe begone in her separation from husband. When her friends and other ladies tried to impress upon her that a wife should not always accompany her husband, Shukala said that for any noble endeavour, a man would not get any merit, if he was not accompanied by his wife. In order to highlight her point, she quoted the example of a devoted lady Sudeva.

Sudeva was the daughter of Kashi's ruler. She was married to Ikshvaku, the scion of the solar dynasty of Ayodhya. Once Ikshvaku had gone for hunting with his family. While in a thick jungle, he happened to espy a wild boar roaming about with his family as well. As the boar spotted the hunting king, it realized that the trouble was high. So, he instructed his wife and kids to remain hidden in a cave, but they refused, saying: 'There are two courses open for us. First is--- slip away quietly before the hunting king gets our smell.' This option was turned down by that brave boar, who said: 'Fleeing away in the face of the enemy is a cowardly act. I must face this king.' Whereupon his family said: 'In that case, we shall also fight against that king.'

Hunting decided their course of action, the boar perched itself atop a high hill and challenged Ikshvaku for the fight. Soon the fight ensued. Sudeva, the wife of Ikshvaku, was helping her husband and the wife of the boar was doing her own bit with kids to help her husband too. After much bloodshed, Ikshvaku managed to kill the boar. As that boar died, there came a vimana from gandharva's land and took the body away. That boar was actually a gandharva.

After the boar's death, the wife of the beast along with her kids continued to fight. Although, they fought quite bravely, they fainted due to wounds and beat.

Meanwhile, Sudeva was watching their agony. She immediately came forward and put some water down the throat of that female boar. As water trickled down her throat she became conscious. Upon inquiry from Sudeva, she revealed that 'she and her husband (boar), both had been gandharvas, who due to a series of curse had become the boar. When they prayed Indra, the divine chief, assured them that after they get killed by the scion of the solar dynasty, they would get back their original form.' And after a pause the boar's wife requested Sudeva that if she could part with a year's merit she had accrued by being devoted to her husband, she may also quit her body and reach near her husband in the gandharva land. Her request surprised Sudeva. She asked the female boar. 'Why? You are so devoted to your husband. Why should you beg a year's merit from me?' 'It is because you are famous for your wifely devotion to your husband. We all know about it.'

Whereupon Sudeva granted a year's merit she had accrued due to the devotion to her husband and that female boar also got united with its husband in the gandharva land.

Narrating this tale, Shukala said: 'She who is devoted to her husband becomes as pure as to check even the sun's rise as Saivya did. That is why, I am waiting for my husband.'

Saying so, she continued to wait for her husband Krikala. Seeing her unflinching devotion, even Indra grew panicky and sent various Apsaras accompanied by Kamadeva, so that they could entirc Shukala to marry Indra. Despite their best efforts, they failed to make Shukala budge from her stand. Shukala rejected Indra's proposal with pomp and riches promised. At last, the Apsara and Kamadeva retuned empty handed. Shukala remained staunch supporter to her husband.

After a long gap, her husband returned home He confessed that he did a mistake by not taking her along. For, when he was coming back, he was told by a sage that 'a person gets no credit if he undertakes any noble project unaccompanied by his wife. It is both man and woman that form the complete unit in this creation Man alone gets no credit by performing holy acts or doing pilgrimage, if he is not with his wife.' Ultimately, Krikala took his wife along on his second trip to the holy spots. Only then his manes were satisfied. Eventually, having visited all the tirthas and repaying debts to their ancestors, they returned home to dwell happily for the remaining part of their lives. When they quit their mortal coil, they ascended to heaven.'

Concluding the narration, sage Pulastya told Bhishma that 'man alone is never deemed complete. He must marry and produce a child to continue the lineage. His ancestors will only then get satisfied and the decendants repay debt they owe to their life. Oh Bhishma! Your case was different as you remain unmarried to keep your father's wish fulfilled. There was yet another father in history, who had once borrowed the youth from his young son to enjoy the sensual delights. He was Yayati.'

3. The Story of Yayati

Yayati was the son of Raja Nahusha, who had once been appointed as Indra, owing to his noble deeds. The position of Indra become vacant when due to some curse the real Indra had to leave his place in heaven and pass life incognito in a pond. Since the divine throne could not have remained vacant for long, the gods consulted sages, seers and Brahma and ultimately the ruler of the earth, Nahusha became the divine chief.

Having received this exalted position, Nahusha wants his son Yayati should also perform such noble deeds as to succeed him as Indra later on. In order to guide Yayati, he sent his divine charioteer, Matali to bring his son to heaven. Reaching earth Matali conveyed his father's desire and asked Yayati to come along to heaven. But, Yayati refused to go, as it was imperative to shun the human body and acquire a divine body. Yayati said : 'Why should I quit this mortal coil, which made me do many a noble deed. This physical body in human form one gets by the blissing of lord Vishnu. Moreover having existence in this body, I can get heaven or hill in accordance with one's good or bad deeds. Also this body gives me an opportunity to go direct to Vaikuntha, the realm of Supreme lord Vishnu. Even if one commits sins, one can get redemption from them through this body only.' And Yayati categorically refused bodily to go heaven.

Yayati proved to be a noble king in all respect. He spread the devotion of lord Vishnu, which made people free of woes and meritorious. Yayati's noble rule began to be lauded by even the gods. Dharma raja himself told Indra about Yayati's flawless administration. In order to test his commitment to righteousness, Indra asked Kamadeva and Rati to go down to Yayati's dance chamber and test his self-control. There Yayati was found wanting as he fell for that danseuse who was actually Rati. Yayati became mad after her and rushed behind to enjoy life with her.

But the problem was that by that time Yayati had become quite old and hence incapable for enjoying sensual delights in the company of a young woman. He then decided to summon his young sons and ask them to lend their youth to them. The eldest son, Taru refused and Yayati cursed him to become a great sinner. The second son Yadu also refused. He too was cursed by his father to pass life in the Kumbhipaak hell. His third son Puru accepted to lend his youth out to his father. With the result, Yayati made Puru his official successor.

Getting again youthful, Yayati solemnized through

gandharva marriage to that girl (Rati) called Vishala. He became so deeply attached to that lady that his legally wedding wives: Sharmishtha and Devayani became jealous of Vishala. Whereupon Yayati asked Puru to slay his wives, but the obedient son bluntly refused. Now the situation became quite serious. Vishala, in the meanwhile, advised Yayati to the worldly bonds and reach Vishnuloka in her company. On her advice, Yayati formally appointed Puru as the king and returned the youth lent out to him.

Concluding the story, Pulastya told Bhishma that if sons accepted their parents' command, they would surely reap rich benefits. One should always obey one's parents to ensure one's well and better living condition in the next life.

❑ ❑ ❑

C. Swarga-Khanda

Bhishm told Pulastya: 'O great sage! You have made me really wise by enlightening me with these stories. I want to hear more such stories.' Pulastya replied: 'Now, I tell you some more episodes which shall make you quite knowledgeable.' He then continued to enlighten Bhishma with following episodes and stories.

Once Sootaji reached Naimisha Kshetra. He was received warmly by sage Shaunaka and other sages. They sought Sootaji to tell them about various holy spots, the stages of life, the duties of the members of different caste people.

Sootaji said: 'Man is God's best creation. He belongs to the most advanced species. He has five sense organs and five organs of action. On the top of it, he has mind. Man leads his life to the best of his ability in this creation with the help of these eleven sources of perception. He is the sole representative of lord Almighty, who has made him wise enough to carve his life out in the best condition. This whole creation has made of three basic gunas called Sattva, Rajas and Tamas. One gets life according to the qualities of the guna dominating him. This whole creation is made of five basic elements : sky, wind, water, fire and the earth. It is these five elements and three basic gunas that go to create four varieties of men: Brahmin, Kshatriya, Vaishya and Shoodra. Among these five elements, the earthy element forms the base, because it has five perceptive modes: Shabda, Sparsha, Roopa, Rasa and Gandha.[2] The water element has only four of them minus the gandha (smell). The element

---

2. Roughly, they represent the capacity to catch sound (Shabda), touch (Sparsh) Roopa (form), Rasa Itaste) and Gandha (smell).

of fire has only three: Shabda, Sparsh and Roopa, the air-element has Shabda and Sparsh; while sky element has only one perceptive mode Sparsh.'

Soota ji said further that in the entire process of creation 'Bharata is the best region. Bharata has many famous seven mountain ranges called Malaya, Mahendra, Sahya, Shaktiman, Vindhya, Paripatra and Rukshwaan. The famous rivers of India (Bharata or the Indian peninsula) are Ganga, Saraswati, Godavari, Yamuna, Narmada, Vitasta, Vipasha, Vetravavati, Iravati, Gomati, Sarayu, Cauvery, Vidisha and Shipra. The famous section of this region are: Panchala, Shurasena, Matsya, Kaushala, Bhoja, Sindhu, Utkala, Kalinga, Avanti, Magadha, Kerala, Karnataka, Konkana, Malava, Aabheera, Saurashtra, which house distinct races of the people.'

'In Indian peninsula, the time cycle stands divided into four Ages: Satya, Treta, Dwapara and Kaliyuga. In the last Age, i.e. Kaliyuga, the life span of man remains rather short People die early. In the Krita (Satya Yuga), man remains by nature noble In Treta, man tends to become more influenced by the Rajo Guna. In Dwapara Yuga, the cross-breed generation dominate, which in Kali Yuga, the rogues and wicked people abound the earth.'

Telling about the famous teerthas, Sootaji extolled the virtues of the holy spot of Pushkar. He says that this one spot gives merit equivalent to 10,000 teertha's merit to the dweller in the region. Those go to these holy sports must lead a pious life, if they wish to derive merit. They must perform yajna, feed brahmins and lead a contented life. In the teertha of Pushkara, dwells the creator Brahma along with Aditya, Vasu and Rudra. Those who go there and lead a pious life have their desires fulfilled automatically. Any penance performed at the holy places gets the performer manifold merits. In Pushkar, there are beautiful ponds and hermitages and bathing in these banks, one gets beyond remain like an ascetic. His duties should be: study of the Vedas, begging alms and serving his mentor. The student should remain totally celebrate and do all his actions when his crown-lock is being tied in a knot. It is believed that untied crown-locks knot results in the person getting no merit no matter what he does. The ideal life course for a Brahmin is indulging in self-study, offering oblution to the departed ancestors and then having food and always moving in a high company of the noble brahmins. The student (Brahmin or Batuk) must disclose his name and father's name and gotra before meeting any respectable persons. Among the respectable persons are counted parents, senior brothers, maternal uncles, grand-father, grand mother, grand maternal parents, mentor and his wife, senior sisters. Whenever one muls them one must show full respect to them. The youngers should respectfully greet the elders but it shouldn't be the other way round. Also, whenever they greet a Brahmin, they must add the prefix *Swasti* before addressing them. The hierarchy of the society in the ascending order is Shudra, Vaishya, Kshatriya and Brahmin. A Brahmin is most adorable to all like Agni is the guru for the twice-born; Brahmin is a natural mentor for other castes.

The social hierarchy is determined with the help of following parameters given in the descending order. Vidya (knowledge), Karma (action), Aayu (age), Sambandha (relationship) and Vitta (money). As is apparent, he who is learned and knowledgeable gets the highest position which the one with riches gets the last priority. Sootaji further clarifies that the ability of being learned covers all deficiencies. If one is learned scholar, at once, he becomes most adorable for the people of the society. However, one consideration should always be borne in mind that one should always make way to a king, a Brahmin, a woman, the one who is carrying load, the one who is weak and emaciated, a celibate, and an ascetic. That is, they should always get precedence over others.

Sootaji then described the bounden duties for all the castes.

A Brahmin celibate should always wash hands and feet before partaking food. He should thoroughly first rinse mouth and never misuse the shade of a tree, a platform of the well, or river, green grass, a ruin, a garden, a highway etc., for his personal convenience. He should deem all women as adorable as his mother and regard others' riches as good as a clod of earth. These are the duties for those who are still in the Brahmacharya Ashram.

He then narrated the duties for those in the grihastha ashram (family life). In this stage of life, he should care for his earning, arranging provisions for the family. It is the most trying stage of life, in which one has to be very guarded. One has to do all his worldly duties without flouting the norms of propriety. He should care for upholding the Dharmic tenets. Although, he should pay attention to his body health yet not at the cost of other's convenience. He had to maintain Dharma and the ordained rituals with seriousness. It is a trying stage because, one had to look after selfish needs yet maintain his casteist duties, as well. This stage should begin with the aspirant taking permission from his mentor to marry a beautiful and an auspicious girl. He should copulate with his wife, three days after her menses. The lunar dates Shashthi (sixth), Ashthami, Chaturdashi and Poornima or Amavasya are the forbidden dates for copulation. A good family man should perform yajnas, as directed by his mentor while always maintaining good contact with noble people. He must deem his guest to be as adoreable as a deity. He should have abundant forgiveness for all beings. The basic qualities of the best family men are Kshama (forgiveness), Daan (liberal alms giving), Daya (kindness), Satya nishtha (always being truthful) and Shanti (peaceful outlook) for all. He should never have any infatuation for any vice. He should enjoy the worldly delights with a sense of renunciation. He who is philanthropic for all the beings given to learning Vedas and remaining a true devotee of lord Vishnu are the symptoms of a good family man

Under no condition, a family man should partake the food offered by a Shoodra. It is believed that one who eats Shoodra's food becomes a veritable Shoodra himself. Apart from the food borrowed from the Shoodra, an ideal family man should not have food with or from a king, a dancer, a cobbler, a prostitute, a thief or an eunuch. Because, eating his food with or from them would pollute his soul. Also, he should not have food prepared by a woman under menses. If he eats such food, he would have his age span reduced.

He should never ditch a Brahmin, a guest, or misbehave with a cow. Neither should be indulge in back-biting against them or in any way damaging threw interest.

He shouldn't be jealous, infatuated or unduly concerned about any vice. He should stay clear of these foul feelings and remain engrossed in what is best for his family or his self.

The third stage of life is called Vanaprastha Ashrama. This is the stage (around 60 years of his age) when he should renounce his worldly pursuits and go to the woods for worshipping God. He shouldn't take his wife along and leave her with his sons. He may take his wife along, should it be not possible. He should live like a celebate ascetic without indulging in any kind of worldly pleasures during stay in the woods. He who doesn't live like a celebrate n this stage of life is sure to fall down below the level of propriety. Unless one quits one's worldly or sensual attractions, there is no sense in his entering Vanaprastha Ashram. He should dwell in a small hut made by himself. Sleep on the floor and weather all the travails of nature without losing his composure.

After Vanaprastha Ashrama comes the Sannyasa

Ashram. This is a very specific stage of life. Those who are willing to spiritually and morally develop their contact with the Almighty, should enter it. Sannyasa itself means even placement with all (Sam + Nyasta). It means that for a Sannyasi, a clod of earth or a piece of gold, his own son or a piece of log should engender identical feeling. This stage's prerequisite is the person's developing total aversion for world or mundane things. Sannyasa is believed to be of three categories: Gyan Sannyasa, Veda Sannyasa and Karma Sannyasa. When the aspirant becomes totally immune to all kinds of worldly attraction, infatuations and affections, one becomes a Gyan Sannyasi. Veda Sannyasi is that person who remains absorbed in the studies of the Vedas, getting above all predictions and prejudices. And he who offers all his actions and their consequences to lord the Almighty and remains alive with no reward of any action is called Karma Sannyasi. Such man should stay on the lap of Nature, near some holy spots with no ill-will for any one. The Sannyasi shouldn't stay permanently and move about all the time. Only during the rainy reason, they can stay at a particular place, but unattached with the local conditions. They should even beg for food and enrich their knowledge by going to different places.

Sootaji says that the real karma yogi is that person who does all the action as ordained in each stage of life. Such man gets beyond the cycle of life and death, after quitting his mortal coil.

It is believed that the greatest hurdle in total devotion to God in a man's path is the love of a woman. It is due to her that even the gods and high sages are trapped in her love. It is the woman, who clouds a man's perception and appears as the real source of happiness. Attraction for woman makes the man lose his discretionary sense, all knowledge and his belief. One should always be wary of her. Although woman is not an uncontrollable obsession for man, she appears as the ultimate deviation point in a man's life Sootaji further emphasized that love for woman and love for god will go together. Scriptures are full of the episodes, highlighting this basic weakness of man. It is by listening to the discourse of saints and seers that one can overcome this biggest hurdle is man's path towards self-realization. Discretion is the essence of knowledge and knowledge is the essence of Dharm. One should always reason the consequences of one's deeds, which is very true in the field of his inclination for the sexual delights. The gods also know about this weakness of man. That is why, the divine chief Indra always uses the Apsaras to deviate one from one's path. Even the great sages like Narada were found wanting in their dealing with women. Even Lord Shankara also fell into Mohini's charms.

Sootaji says that lord the Almighty doesn't need to act, but for showing man the righteous path. He often incarnates and performs actions. One should always concentrate one's mind to the form of lord Vishnu, who is eternal and infallible existence alone in this entire creation. Should one look for riches and sensual delights, one is likely to fall. Remember that no matter what one earns in this impermanent world will remain here only. No one can take along even an iota of gold when one goes to the other world. Hence hoarding is the most abominable act. One should use a commodity as much as one needs. For, there is enough in the world for man's need, but there shall never be enough for his greed. If one has excess wealth, it should be utilized in building temples of God and doing charity for others' welfare. Money is what it does. This being the way, he who follows the dictats and passes each stage of life in total conformity with what the Scriptures say; not only one lives happily, but also ensures happiness in the next life. He who believes lord Vishnu to be the final object of worship in this world ensures al happiness, not only for himself and family, but for all beings of this creation.

❑ ❑ ❑

D. Brahma Khanda

[In this chapter, the dialogue between Shaunaka and Sootaji is given which portrays important Vratas, extremely useful to the devotees or the man.]

Having heard in details about Karma Yoga, or the rituals of leading an ideal life, Bhishma sought to learn from sage Pulastya about what a man should and what shouldn't do. He particularly asked about the criminal acts, or those heinous acts, which were held most sacrilegious in scriptures. Pulastya quoted often a dialogue between Shaunaka and Sootaji to highlight these points. This pair also being referred to the dialogue between Jaimini and the great Sage Vedavyasa to emphaise his narration.

In Kali yuga, human life span shrinks and becomes quite small. Moreover, it is full of pains-sorrows and other troubles. When Jaimini asked Vyasa as to how could a person of Kali yuga get redemption from these travails, Vyasji replied 'only through a dedicated worship of God and listening the discourses of noble saints and other God-realised men. Whereupon Jaimini asked: 'Oh great Sage! In this Kali yuga, there is so much of chicanery and perjury that it becomes difficult to identify a noble person.' Vyasji listed then the following criteria to judge as to who is noble, and who is not. The noble pure-hearted and noble persons are those who are,

(i)   Not affected by sexual desire, anger, infatuation or greed,

(ii)   Totally non-violent and treating things with even affection.

(iii) Give respect to brahmins and Universe

(iv) Well-versed in Scriptures and the Vedas

(v) Religiously observant of the holy Vratas like Ekadashi, Janmashthami and Radhashthami.

(vi) Surrounded ever by god-fearing and honest persons

(vii) Devoted to lord Vishnu or Krishna and devoid of any kind of ill-will for any body.

These are the tell-tale symptoms of a noble or good persons. But, whether one be noble or evil, if one honesty sings lord's songs and performs His worship devotedly also attains salvation.

Vyasji then said that one is able to perform an honest worship of lord provided one has not committed any of the heinous acts. These are ten in numbers and are called: "Nama-Aparaadha'. They are listed below:

(i) Criticizing the good and the noble,

(ii) Discerning a deliberate difference between lord Shiva and lord Vishnu,

(iii) Disobeying one's Guru or other seniors of that category,

(iv) . Indulging in calumny against the Scriptures,

(v) Deriving commercial benefit out of glorifying lord Supreme,

(vi) Changing the rules and rituals of Dharma, Vrata and yajna etc., for personal convenience,

(vii) Indifference to chanting lord's holy names,

(viii) Getting ever involved in physical materials and caring ever for sensual gratification,

(ix) Having cruel or unkind behaviour for others,

(x) Showing hostility or animosity towards Brahmins.

Until the person remains involved in any of the above mentioned acts, s(he) cannot worship God honestly. And even if s(he) does the person would not get any merit for them. Because whatever s(he) may earn through noble acts may be lost in the profane activities. It is tantamount to filling a tank having as big a hole in the bottom as the pipe that is pouring water into the tank. As a person gets away from these dirty or heinous acts, he realizes their deep level of profanity. Then a pristine glow emerges in his heart and he starts observing what is good for him. Recession from these acts creates a longing for doing something noble. He realizes that no matter what name one gives to one god, in reality all roads lead to one entity – that is all caring and ever manifest lord the Supreme.

The chanting of lord's holy names is often compared with one having a holy dip in the confluence of Ganga, Yamuna and the invisible Saraswati – The Sangam. One must have the urge in oneself to worship God or move in the noble company. Unless that urge surfaces, no artificial or forced acts can bring solace.

In this context, Sootaji quoted a dialogue between lord Narayan and Lord Shankar. Once the peripatetic sage Narada happened to reach the mount Mandarachala for having darshan of lord Shankara. Lord Shiva reverentially welcomed the sage and inquired the purpose of his visit. Narada sought lord Shiva to dwell on describing the great glory of lord Vishnu. Lord Shiva replied that 'it is colossal that I can't fathom, nevertheless, I tell you whatever I know. Situated amidst 1,25,000 hills, there is a holy spot called Badarikashram. On a hill near it dwell two great sages called Nara and Narayana. They have internal form and they collectively manifest in the form of lord Vishnu or lord Krishna. This place Badarikashram remains snow clad when the Sun remain titled southwards from its axis, which is called Dakshinayana. As such, Narayana is the supreme deity among all. Once, he condescended to have me his Darshan and asked me which boons I desired. I have asked for two boons: one, unflinching faith in him and becoming his chief devotee and the other – becoming capable enough to grant emancipation to my own devotees. He was gracious enough to allow me both boons. It is on account of that boon that I am known as Narayana's chief devotee. Despite being ash-covered with dry and untidy locks, I have become capable of granting release from the mundane travails to my devotee O Narada! My lord Narayana becomes happy with even little worship, if genuine.

Narada then asked Shiva about the various Vratas (fasts) which also make one go beyond mundane bonds. In order to explain the effect of certain fasts, Shiva narrated a tab to Narada.

Long long ago, there was a ruler of the earth named Raja Harishchandra. By virtue of his Yoga sadhana, he could fly in his vehicle. Once, he spotted the child sage Sanat Kumar perched atop a golden hill. Out of curiosity, the king came near him and sat before him hand bound. Sanat Kumar found him quite curious to know something. When the child sage allowed him to speak, the king said: 'O Sage! I have now much wealth and property in my possession. I am a chakravarty (king). What were my deeds in the consequence of which I received so much property and authority and what should I do so that this kind of riches and power ever remain with me?

Sanat Kumar replied: 'O Great King! In your previous life, you were an honest and god-fearing trader (Vaishya). Since you had become indifferent to all wealth, your brethren had almost ostracized you. Gradually, you remained all alone. Although, your wife tried to be honest with you, there came a stage when she also left you. This had made you leave your home in utter penury. Reaching near a pond filled with many lotus flowers, you began to survive by selling off those flowers. Once you reached Kashi with your stock of flowers, you couldn't get hunger. Carrying the load, you roamed about everywhere and eventually reached near a Mutt. You have found the ruler of Kashi, Indradyumna celebrating the festival of Janmashthami with his daughter. They used to observe strict fast of Janmashthami and worship lord Krishna quite frequently. You offered flowers to that Krishna idol and happened to pass the entire night worshipping lord Krishna by singing devotional songs. The princess was impressed with your unflinching devotion who observed your offering flowers had completed the ritual of her worship. Feeling obliged, she tried to grant you something in return in the form of money and other costly items, but you just refused to accept anything in return. The princess also offered you some royal food. Despite your starving for the day, you often refused that offer. This way you have made great sacrifice and refused the food despite being hungry. Since your devotion was not guided by any desire of return, you earned great merit. In return, you become such a great king in this life. Your present position is the result of that worship on that holy day of Vrat.

'But what should I do now to continue enjoying, all these comforts and benefits?" asked the king, adding 'please tell me in detail about the ritual worship the devotee should perform on the day of Janmashthami. Sanat Kumar replied: 'Now, I enlighten you on the ritual worship on the day of Janmashthami, as ordained by creator Brahma.' Then he spelt on the formal worship.

On the day of Janmashthami which falls on the 8th lunar day of the dark half of the month Shravan, the devotee should bathe early in the morning with water having black sesame (til seeds) soaked overnight. He should bathe with five pitchers of water. Taking a fresh earthen pitcher, clean it with milk and other materials and put five costly gems into that pitcher. Annoint it with the mark of sandalwood paste making a half-moon and the Nakshatra Rohini. The god (Krishna) on that day should be clad in white clothes. Light incense before the idol and sing devotional songs for the day and night. Celebrate the lord's advent to the mortal world at midnight, and offer pancake as the prasad. Concluding the description, Sanat Kumar said: 'When you did that worship unknowingly, you became a king (chakravarty). Now, if you do it knowingly, you will surely get not only lord Krishna's unflinching devotion, but final release from this cycle of birth and death. You will attain emancipation, if you observe the vrata with full ritual.'

When Parvati heard these Krishna-Janmashthami details from lord Shankara, she asked her master as to which other months are dear to lord Krishna apart from Shravan, the month of birth. Lord Shankara said: 'O Blessed one! Lord Krishna has special liking for Amla fruit and Tulsi (basil) leaves. Since in the month of Kartika, all holy teerthas stay at the root of Tulsi, Lord Krishna also loves that month. Planting a Tulsi plant and performing marriage on the Ekadashi Day of that month is very auspicious. He who does so gets special blessings from Lord Krishna. It is said that all holy teerthas, gods and seers always converge around the Tulsi plant in the month of Kartika.'

Telling an old story, lord Shankara highlighted the great importance of the 12-syllable mantra: 'Om Namo Bhagwate Vaasudevaaya'. The story is as follows.

Long long ago in the town of Karaveerapur in the Sahayadri region, there lived a very religious Brahmin Dharma Datta. He had a knack of chanting the holy mantra forever: 'Om Namo Bhagwate Vaasudevaaya' with his every breath. On some day in the month of Kartika, he performed a very difficult vrata on the Ekadashi day and remained awake the whole night. He left the temple with pooja material and prasad after worship in the last hour of the that tithi. He happened to come across a very deadly figure. The person had blood-hot bulging eyes, dry and parched lips and protruded eerie teeth. Dharma Dutta became panic stricken and threw a few drops of holy water while chanting favourite mantra, to keep that demonic figure. As the drops of water touched the demon's body, sins of demons were dissolved in that water. Instead, there emerged a woman who bowed to Dharma Datta and said: "O Brahmin! This water has destroyed my sins, now I have very pious thoughts. I got this dreadly form, owing to my own great misdeed in the previous birth. In my previous birth, I was the wife of a poor Brahmin. I was very harsh on my husband and everybody condemned him, for his almost beggar like penury. I would say most piercing things and would find one excuse and other for fighting. At last, getting sick of me, my husband tried to get a second wife. But, I deliberately consumed poison in order to involve my husband in a murder case. Yama's accountant did no good deed in my file, when I reached Yama Loka. My past deeds were examined, and they put me in the species of demons. Since then, I have been living in this deadly form.'

Dharma Dutta felt pity on that women and thought as to how she could get redemption. Since that woman was in the species of a demon, she couldn't have performed a vrata or other holy acts. So, first be thought that she should be redeemed from the unholy species. He took a mental resolve: 'I willingly grant half of the merit that may have accrued to me on account of my doing that vrata of this holy Ekadashi of the month of Kartika.' He sprinkled some water on that woman while thinking so and loudly chanted his favorite mantra: 'Om Namo Bhagwate Vaasudevaaya' into her ears. Immediately, she became a very pious lady with a golden body and bowing reverentially to Dharma Dutta went to Brahma's realm.

This story reveals that those who perform vrata in the Kartika month have their sins dissolved instantly. It is because Kartik month is associated with Tulsi. Tulsi is being inseperably attached with lord Krishna or Vishnu. The most prominent day of this month is Deepavali. On the day before the Deepavali, i.e., on Trayodashi, the devotee should kindle lamp in the name of Yamaraj (Yama-Diya), which should be placed at the threshold of his house. He should pray for getting riddance from death on the next day morning He should chant the names of Dharma Raj, Mrityu, Vivaswaan, Antaka, Parmeshthu, and Yamaraja, while pronouncing *Namah* term with every uttered name after bathing in the morning. The same kind of lamp should be put near every water course around the house and in the temples of lord Vishnu, Brahma and Shiva on the moonless day, i.e., on the Amavasya, the devotee should bathe and worship has departed ancestors (the manes) and should feed noble and learned Brahmins. He should then worship the goddess of riches, Bhagawati Lakshmi Devi with the prayer: 'O great goddess! Grant me all riches with total mental satisfaction. May my desires be fulfilled.' After saying so, he should distribute sweets among friends and celebrate the festival of Deepavali by lighting lamps.

On the Deepavali day, the worship of Raja Bali should also be performed. Take five coloured pastes including honey and paint a demonic figure. Worship it by lighting incense etc. If he does so, his prosperity would remain enriched for the entire year.

On the next day of Deepavali, after his morning chanting rituals and worshipping Yamaraja, he should go to his sister's place and give her gifts along with dakshina. This way duly propitiated, Yamaraja would make both his sister and he, free of the fear of death. Deepavali festival should thus be celebrated ensuring prosperity and the grant of riches. [Curiously enough, the Deepavali worship has no mention of lord Ganesha in this purana. May be, since Ganesha later joined the rank of the Aryan worship pantheon, his worship was associated with goddess Lakshmi later, when Ganesha came to be recognized as the Vighneshwara].

Sootaji enlightened the assembled sages in the Naimisharanya by quoting various dialogues between lords Shankara-Parvati and other seers. Emphasising on lord Vishnu's worship, Sootaji said that those who keep fasts on the holy days especially in the month of Kartika, enjoy unrestrained prosperity and happiness.

❑ ❑ ❑

E. Patala Khanda

[Curiously enough, this section of the *Padma Purana* mentions almost the entire Rama-Katha alongwith some other details of Rama's doings which are not available in the Rama's story told either in the Ramayana by Valmiki or by Goswami Tulsidas in his celebrated magnum opus *Ramacharita Manas*. Some of the stories provide the necessary fillip to the standard Rama-katha and hence are quite interesting].

Bhishma was delighted to listen to many stories told by sage Pulastya, while profusely quoting Sootaji, Shankara and other celebrated gods and sages. But, their stories whetted his appetite further, for listing more such revealing stories. He sought Putastya now to relate the doings of Lord Rama to him with details. Pulastya obliged by first briefly summarizing the entire Rama's story in a paragraph and highlighted about *Shambaka Vadha*. He recounts Rama's story is detail with much of the flash-back from this anecdote. [This flash back technique has been employed in a masterly way and perhaps the modern film makers could get a lesson or two from the techniques of Padma Purana).

After having slayed Ravan and his demon hosts, Rama returned Ayodhya with Sita and Lakshman and started 'ruling majestically. [His rule is believed to be an ideal rule even in the modern times Gandhiji often equated 'Rama-Rajya' with an ideal rule].

Some day, a Brahman carrying the dead body of his young son arrived while Rama was on his throne in his court. He said: 'Lord Rama! How come this unusual event happened? My young son expired even when I am alive. If people suffer such unusual and heart-breaking events, surely it is on account of some misdeed done by the king. Now, you're the king and it is your duty to relive my boy. He expired untimely, because of some misdeed done by you. As far as I remember, I have not done any thing wrong. It is then the king's misdeed whose consequences the people had to suffer. So, lord, please undo this grievous damage.'

Rama, the king, was aghast.. He wondered how could such a thing happen in his rule. In order to probe further on this dreadful happening, Rama spoke to his mentor, Vasishtha, Narada arrived there suddenly. 'Lord Rama', Narada said: 'Such events shouldn't happen in your rule. You must find out the cause behind it and nip such causes in the budding stage. Else, they may set the wrong precedence.'

On consultation with Vasishtha, Rama learnt that such deaths should occur when some rule of law was flouted. After much inquiry, it was learnt that there was a Shoodra boy called Shambuka, who was under penance. Now, as the Shoodras, by the Scriptural laws, were not enlitted to perform tapas or study Vedas, Shambuka's penance definitely flouted the holy law. Hence, the untimely death of that brahmin's son.

Getting this knowledge about Shambuka, lord Rama went out in his chariot to prevent him from indulging in the practices reserved for the high castes– brahmins, kshatriyas, vaishyas are only entitled to read the Vedas and perform tapas (penance or vratas). But, when Shambuka refused to obey the royal order and insisted on doing so, Rama had no option, other than to behead him. [After all the norms of the propriety had to be preserved].

As he killed Shambuka, the dead brahman's son was relived and all chanted slogan in Rama's glory.

But, now Rama was in pensive mood. He thought: 'the truth is that I am also not totally sinless. I have murdered Ravana, Kumbhakarna etc, who were Brahmin. Don't I carry the stigma of brahminicide on my head?' In order to find some solace, he went to sage Agastya's hermitage.

As lord Rama reached there, Agastya heartily welcomed him and presented a beautiful piece of ornament to the lord. Although lord Rama said, it wasn't just for the king to accept gifts from sages, Agastya said: 'Accept this king! I give you, because it has a beautiful anecdote behind it.' Lord Rama accepted the gift and said: 'Please tell me the anecdote' and Agastya obliged thereby.

Once sage Agastya was under penance inside a dense forest, he found a beautiful vimana (aerial vehicle) alighting near a comely pond and a beautiful god-like person came out of that. The person then took a dead body out, hidden in the bushes and began to devour it piece by piece. Agastya was aghast. That divine person and this abominable act eating a dead body! He couldn't check himself and asked that person the reason behind his abominable act. That person narrated his story.

In previous life, there was a king, Vasudeva of Vaidarbhaka kingdom. He had two sons named Shweta and Surath. After Vaasudeva, Shweta was made the king. But he didn't find such ruling of interest, so giving the throne to his brother Sura. Shweta went under penance in the jungle. He was under penance for many thousand years and finally went to heaven. But even when in heaven, he always felt hungry and thirsty. When he asked Brahma as to what was the reason behind, Brahma replied: 'In heaven, you get what you give on the earth. Since you gave no food or drink to anyone, you have to remain thirsty and hungry. But now, owing to your high merits, you can't get back to earth. You have to remain in heaven. However, in order to solve your hunger and thirst related problem, I have made one provision. Your deceased mortal core is still under-composed, lying in the forest, where you breathed your last. You may go there and eat your dead body and drink water from the pond. You have to do this daily.' After a pause, that person said: 'I am that fellow, Sbweta. Brahma told me that the day I meet the divine sage Agastya, I shall get rid of this filthy food and shall get good food in heaven.'

The sage said: 'I am Agastya!' Shweta was delighted to have that curse ending and after presenting a beautiful ornament to the sage, departed heavenwards. 'This is that divine ornament,' Agastya said: 'Please adorn that, as it is meant for you.' Lord Rama accepted that gratefully and said: 'O great Sage! I have come here with a specific issue that is troubling my mind? And then lord Rama told about Shambuka and the rank of brahminicide that was troubling him after his slaying Ravan and Kumbhakarn, who were actually brahmin.

But Agastya took another view. He said: 'Raja Rama! Remember that a Brahmin is Brahman only, when he behaves like a Brahmin. Killing scores of innocents and abducting other's wife is not a brahminical act. Ravan and Kumbhakarn were in no way Brahmin any more. Their birth in a Brahmin family was an accident. Until one proves one's brhaminhood by his act and conduct, one cannot be a so.' Then in order to make lord Rama happy and relieved of the thought of being a culprit, sage Agastya asked him to perform an Ashwamedha Yajna. 'Once, you perform this yajna, you shall feel happy as all your sins done knowingly or unknowingly shall be destroyed'. Sage Agastya told lord Rama that the latter's ancestor Dilip had acquired total

Siddhi by performing the Ashwamedha yajna. He also quoted many examples of Manu, Sagar, Marut and Yayati to give him his final advice.' Return to Ayodhya and perform the Ashwamedha Yajna with the cooperation of your brothers. I bless you that you shall be such a king, who shall also be quoted as an ideal ruler.'

Lord Rama returned happily to Ayodhya and consulted his brothers about performing the Yajna. Bharat often said: 'O king! The whole creation is already under your suzerainty. Instead of performing the Yajna, you should ensure that all you territory should have the rule of righteousness (Dharma) only. That would be a bigger achievement than your performing the Yajna.' Lord Rama liked his suggestion and campaigned of having *Dharma Rajya* first by installing the idol of Vamana at Kanya kubja.'

When Bhishma inquired about the installation of Vamana idol in Kanyakubja, Pulastya told him the following anecdote.

One day lord Rama wondered: 'Although I had made Vibhishana, the ruler of Lanka, I have not cared to see whether he is having the righteous rule or continuity with the demonic rule.'. When lord Rama told Bharata about it, Bharata suggested that they should go to Lanka and see what Vibhishana was doing there. Entrusting the rule of Ayodhya to Lakshmana, lord Rama moved towards Lanka in his Pushpaka Vimana accompanied by Bharata and his other lieutenants.

On their way, they thought it necessary to meet Sugreeva also. While going to Kishkinda, lord Rama showed Bharata the important places in his previous southward journey like the place where consort Sita was abducted, Jatayu was killed etc. They were grandly welcomed by Sugreeva, Angad, Jambavanta and the monkey and bear hosts. The sages also came to meet them. When Sugreeva learnt about their destination—Lanka, he also joined the party. Vibhishana was delighted to receive an advance information from Hanuman about Lord Rama's revisit to Lanka. When they reached Lanka, there came many stalwarts of demons, sages and seers etc. to welcome the brigade of lord Rama. He was presented a score of costly gift items. Kaikesi, mother of Vibhishana expressed her desire to meet lord Rama, who obliged all. Sarama, the wife of Vibhishan also came to inquire about Sita's welfare.Lord Rama stayed there for three days. When he was about to depart, Vayudeva came and suggested that the huge Vamana idol lying in Lanka should be taken along and installed in Kanyakubya (the present Kannauj in Madhya Pradesh). Lord Rama accepted the request. When he left Lanka, Vibhishana convinced lord Rama that he was ruling over Lanka following the Aryan ideals, and not according to the demon-ethics. But, he complained that many rogues used to come from north to disturb his administration. So, he requested lord Rama to break the bridge, he built earlier. Lord Rama had it broken to pieces. They left Lanka in the pushpaka vimana and reached Mathura via Pushkara. Mathura was in charge of Shatrughna, who welcomed the whole brigade. Staying in Mathura for a couple of days, lord Rama reached Kanyakubja, on the banks of river Ganga and had the idol of Vamana duly installed. He declared that he who worshipped Vamana at Kanyakubja would get much merit. Lord Rama distributed the wealth he had received in Lanka to the learned brahmins. At Kanyakubja, lord Rama bade adieu to Sugreeva and others and arrived back in Ayodhya.

Having established the rule of righteousness all over the region under his control, lord Rama consulted his brothers about performing the Ashwamadha Yajna. All of them agreed. The yajna was commenced with much fanfare and the consecrated horse was let loose under the command of Shatrughna and the Raghava (lord Rama's) brigade. The horse had a plaque of gold with clear instructions that the horse symbolized lord Rama's authority. Those who opposed it would have to fight with the army, while those who allowed the horse to be tied their domain must pay due tax to Raja Rama.

Shatrughna was assisted by Bharata's son Pushkala, Hanuman and other stalwarts of the Kaushala brigade.

As the brigade following the consecrated horse moved ahead, the demon Vidyumali created suchdarkness that nothing was visible. Moreover, the sky began to rain blood and pus. In that confusion, the consecrated horse looked quite lost. Shatrughna was worried. He went out with soldiers to search for the horse. On the way, he learnt that Maya was thus the creation of that demon Vidyumali. Shatrughna used his divine weapons to diffuse the confusion and killed Vidyawati. Eventually, his horse was found and the party moved ahead.

Rama's brigade led by the consecrated horse moved ahead to reach a powerful kingdom called Devapur. Its ruler Raja Veeramani was a religious and prosperous king. He had a son called Angad, who was a lecher. He was enjoying in an orchard at the outskirts of the town in the company of beautiful dames. The dames, when they espied the horse, fell for that beautiful stud. They inquired Angada to overpower the horse and put it in his stable. Angada knew that his father was an arch devotee of lord Shankar's Rudra form. When he tied the horse in the stable and told has father Veeraman about it, the king expressed his displeasure at this silly act. Even when lord Shankara was asked, the great lord said plainly: 'Don't expect any favour from me if you take up cudgels against lord Rama's army. He is my chosen deity as well.' But Angad insisted on continuing the fight for justice, according to his principle once a Kshatriya took a stand, he must uphold that. However, when Hanuman heard about his forces being challenged by lord Shankara's devotee, he expressed dismay. 'I have always believed that lord Shankara deemed himself as lord Ram's arch devotee, how come his devotees have slain Pushkala and Shatrughna.' Lord Shankara replied you have heard rightly, but I was helpless as my devotees were slain by lord Ram's forces. Although, a fierce fight began between the two: the father (Shiva) and the son (Hanuman), soon the fight was stopped by divine intervention. Hanuman then went to the Himalayes to bring the herb *Sanjeevani* to relive the dead. At last with the help of Brihaspati, the divine priest, the desired herb was found and the dead, including Pushkala and Shatrughna relived back to life.

Angada headed to the divine advice and let go of the consecrated horse. Moving ahead, followed by lord Rama's army led by Shatrughna and Hanuman, the horse came close to Valmiki's ashrama. In the precincts of the ashrama, Luv, Sita (Rama's) elder son, was moving around with friends. He was the horse and held its reins. Then the read the 'plaque' declaring royal challenge to all those who attempted to hold the horse. Amused he thought of accepting the challenge as he himself was a brave boy. Although love was advised by his companions not to take up cudgels with the Royal Awadh Army he refused saying: "As a brave Kshatriya, I can't bit this challenge go unaccepted." He held the horse and tied to a titter inside his Ashram.

[While narrating this anecdote, the sage Pulastya goes into flash back and narrates the anecdote of Sita, abandonment by lord Rama following a washerman's admonishing his wife for her stay in a foreigner's house, with the comment that 'I am not lord Rama to accept Sita even though she had passed many nights in captivity of the demon Ravana.' When lord Rama heard of it, he decided to abandon Sita, who was also pregnant. Lakshmana had to do this unpleasant duty of abandoning Sita in the dense jungle. Fortunately, sage Valmiki saw and took her to his heritage, where Sita at due time gave birth to twins [Luv and Kush].

When the soldiers of the royal army saw a mere boy holding the consecrated horse captive, they tried to amicably persuade him to let go the horse. The boy contemptuously laughter at their request the soldiers began to attach the boy and his companions. The boys were no novice. They fought so bravely that the soldiers of the Awadh army had to retreat. They informed Shatrughna and Hanuman about the uncontrollable boys. Whereupon Hanuman and Shatrughan asked the boy to reval his lineage. But Luv answered: 'on the battlefield, one is known by the identity displayed by one's superior weapon weilding. Now start the fight without much ado.'

And then the fight ensued. Luv fought so bravely and intelligently that he managed to knock off the crown from Shatrughna's head. Thus enraged Shatrughna fought very bravely and made that boy Luv lose his consciousness. Luv's fallow boys took their leader to safety of the Ashram, where Sita attended the wounded. By that time Kush, younger brother of Luv, had returned to the hermitage, after visiting the temple of Mahakala. He also attached the Awadh Army. Now, Luv also became fully conscious and both the adolescent brothers made a mincemeat of the attacking soldiers. They made even Shatrughna lose consciousness and made Sugreeva and Hanuman captive, as though they had been an ordinary monkey. But when Sita saw Sugriva and Hanuman, she asked her sons to immediately release the prisoners. Now Sita knew who her sons were fighting against? She criticized her son for their having taken up cudgels against their own father. Whereupon the boys quoted many examples from history to assert that taking up cudgels against father for a genuine cause was no sacrilege. However after much cajoling and coaxing, the boys let go of both Hanuman and Sugreeva along with the horse. Sita made, by dint of her wifely devotion and purity, alive the stain soldiers of lord Rama's brigade. Now having retrieved the horse, Shatrughna alongwith his lieutenants marched back to Ayodhya, triumphantly announcing the victory of their mission. Raja Ram welcomed all are wished to know the details of their mission's accomplishment. Learning about the boys at the hermitage who looked like Raghuvanshis (scion of Raghu's family) lord Ram went to Sage Valmiki's hermitage and requested the sage about telling the details of the wonder boys. Valmiki then told lord Ram about Sita and her begetting two sons and assured king Ram that Sita was as pure as the river Ganga. Lord Ram returned to Ayodhya and ordered Lakshman for bringing the daughter of Janaka back to Ayodhya with her sons. Lakshmana said: 'Since I was the person who had earlier left her amidst jungle all alone, perhaps she may not like to return with him.' But Ram insisted on Lakshman to execute the job. At last, Lakshman went to the hemitage and requested Sita to return. Sita said: 'though I am satisfied with this request made by Lord Ram, I shall not go back to bring dot to his fair glory. However, Luv and Kush can return to their father's place, if they so wished.' But, Luv-Kush also refused. When Lakshman told lord Ram about Sita's opinion, he made Lakshman return to the hermitage and tell Sita of his agony of separation. At last, she agreed and returned to Ayodhya with her sons. Lord Rama accepted her and her two sons lovingly and accomplished the Ashwamedha yajna.[3]

It is said that after the Yajna, lord Ram begana to rule comfortably. At that time, sages and seers including lord Shiva and His spouse had started dwelling at river Sarayu's banks. They sought Jambavant to recount to them the full tale of lord Rama's doings and Jambavant obliged. Beginning from the following episode of Raja Dashrath's life which made him particularly long for progeny.

It so happened that a king cal Saadhya happened to attack Awadh under Raja Dashrath's rule.

The war lasted for 60 days and eventually Dashrath managed to hold the invading king Raja Saadhya as captive. Sadhya had a son called Bhushana. When he found his father imprisoned under Raja Dashrath's captivity, mobilized from the anguish, he attacked Dashrath with the available forces. Dashrath felt pity on that soft bodied princes fighting for his father's release and managed to imprison Bhushan as well without any effort. When both father and son are kept imprisoned, instead of feeling sorry for being so imprisoned, they felt quite happy. Their mutual affection made Dashrath long for begetting a son. Till that time, he was also issue-less. Saadhya told Dashrath that if he observed fast on eleventh lunar day while chanting the holy Mantra: *Om Namo Bhagwate Vaasudevaya* and donated a cow he might beget a son. During this period, the aspirant must worship Keshava's (lord Krishna or Vishnu's) idol

---

3. This twist in the story as given in this Purana is at complete veriance with the story given in the Valmiki Ramayan. According to Valmiki Ramayana, Sita never returned to Ayodhya and had requested the Mother earth to open up so that she could cave in that crevice. She eventually did so and a weeping Ram had to return to Ayodhya with only his two sons Luv and Kush. The Ramayana says that Sita felt so perturbed on observing the father and sons about to fiddle each other with arrows that she chose to quit her mortal coil there. The same story in this Purana is quite amazing, perhaps giving happy end to the saga of lord Rama.

after bathing in pure ghee. Dashrath was impressed with his knowledge and on the advice of his priest started the Putreshthi yajna. Eventually, he got four sons: Rama, Bharata, Lakshman and Shatrughna. Narrating the entire saga of lord Rama from the very beginning, Jambavant regaled the audience with conversationalist and engrossing style. [This Purana recounts the whole story of Rama with little variance from the standard saga of lord Rama Katha.] The varying points are the following:

(i) Raja Janaka had already been assured by lord Shankara that the latter's bow called *Ajagava* was unbreakable by anybody except lord Rama;

(ii) Vishwamitra himself had tried to hand that bow in order to make his attempt to marry Sita. Rest of the story of lord Rama is similar.

This chapter ends with the assertion by sage Pulastya that lord Rama and Shiva are no different, but names of one deity. Then after lord Shiva returned Kailash and lord Rama started ruling ideally.

❏ ❏ ❏

F. Uttara Khanda

Bhishma said: 'O great Sage! The way you have interpreted the spiritual contents enshrined in the small stories that you recounted enriched my knowledge and wisdom greatly. I am looking forward to hearing more such stories from you.' Sage Pulastya then recounted the following anecdotes.

Long ago, great saints and seers assembled in Nemisharanya. Often, the situation arose when my preceptor Vyasji happened to reach there. The sages sought Vedavyasji to confide them about devotion to lord Narayana (Vishnu) and consequences, thereof.

Vedavyas told them that once goddess Sati posed similar question about lord Narayana's devotion and whatever lord Shankara had told them would now be told by him to the sages. Delving on the salient features lord Shiva told her that:

(i)   Total concentration of the mind yields best form of devotion.

(ii)   He who achieves this concentration on lord Vishnu becomes the lord's satvik devotion.

(iii)   Satvik devotion is the best form of any devotion.

(iv)   Those who indulge in this kind of devotion, while getting involved in the sensual delights get the medium quality of devotion.

(v)   Those who indulge in such devotion, while nursing it will for others get the worst form of devotion.

Further enlightening goddess Sati, lord Shankara said that essence of the real devotion is total surrender before the chosen lord. One should remember the god the same way as a thirsty man longs for water, frozen man for fire, fearful man for protection, one desirous of getting a son for a son, those couniqned to darkness for the sun, the greedy for money. Gods value the purity of the sentiments most. Devotion should have no desire for return. For getting lord Narayana's grace, one should not care for offering lots of wealth as money is meaningless for the deity. God sees all and he knows one's hearts feeling. One should never try to hide his feeling before his chosen deity nor should ever attempt to camouflage one's sentiments. Devotion for lord Narayana is the ultimate duty of all the human beings Bhakti provides one strength to swim across this ocean of existence without ever succumbing to the sensual delights. Even, if one gets a little of this devotion, one has his all sins destroyed the same way as a mere fire-ling is enough to destroy the huge stock of dry cotton. Lord Narayana never distinguishes between his devotees, no matter one be a saint or a criminal, king or a pauper. He is attainable to all with even intensity, provided one has pure feeling. He who is ever in communion with the ord becomes a fully realized soul.

Although the devotion to lord Vishnu is of either types: *with form* and *without form*. In fact, the devotion *with form* is a medium to reach *devotion without form*. One attains total coalescence with one's chosen lord Narayana when one reaches that stage. Of course, man is bound by the consequences of previous deed, but it is the purity of feeling that liberates one from bondages. All deeds have one goal, reaching unto lord Keshava. Devotion is preferable over Gyan or Karma Yoga, because it doesn't require any paraphernalia of rituals or knowledge. It needs only total surrender. Although, it is quite difficult to negate everything else including self, yet that is the sure way of attaining Narayana. However, there is other gradation as well. It is believed that:

* Gyan and Yoga path are difficult paths.
* Gyan and Yoga's communion makes one totally concentrated.
* In devotion, there is no logic or argument.

One single requirement is of purity of feelings.

Those who go for Gyan Yoga or Karm Yoga are never able to achieve union with chosen lord. The elimination of sense of identity is a difficult proposition, though it may appear simple. It is believed that *Mamata* (affection or love), 'Ahamta (the sense of I-ness or self identity) and passion (Vasana) are the three most ineliminatable propositions. Ahanta is the hardest nut to crack even among them. That can be achieved only by the total surrender. The crux of devotion is Tat-sukha-suphee' (i.e., only consideration of the deity's happiness at the cost of total surrender of the self. The ideal devotee doesn't care for his own happiness or return. For him (or her), the sole consideration of the deity's happiness.

In order to highlight the glory of devotion, sage Vedavyas sought the child sage Sanat-Kumar to recount the anecdote of slaying of the demon Jalandhar.

The Tale Jalandhar's Slaying:

In ancient times, once the chief of the gods, Indra, with the divine preceptor, Brihaspati, went to have darshan of lord Shiva. In order to test the validity of their faith, Shankar (Shiva) disguised himself as an old and bearded ascetic, and stationed himself at the gate of his dwelling place over the mount Kailash. The chief of the gods, Indra, asked the old ascetic about lord Shankara, he did not reply and pretended as though, he was lost in meditation. Drunk in the wine of his supreme position, arrogant Indra thought as though the old ascetic had deliberately kept quiet to show his contempt to the divine chief. Enraged, Indra hit the silent ascetic with his thunder bolt, but the mystic power of Shiva (the ascetic) blunted the edge of Indra's weapon. Indra's temerity further male the third eye of the ascetic open and a fierce power shot forth from it. At that moment, Brihaspati recognized the reality of that pseudo-ascetic (Shankara) and requested lord Shiva to forgive Indra. Lord Shiva though acceded to the request, but the fire could not be controlled. He took the fire, now in a beacon form, and threw it in the *Ksheera Sagar* (Ocean of Milk), where it landed and immediately assumed the form of a powerful and brilliant male infant. The new-born child began to wail loudly at the shore of the ocean, causing distress even to the guardian of quarters, who informed lord Brahma.

The boy put his arm round the creator and suppressed his throat so powerfully that tears welled up in the eyes of the creator. The creator reached near the boy and took him on to this lap. Seeing his great power, creator gave the boy name: Jalandhar (meaning carried by water). The creator looked at his future and found him to be destined to become the future lord of demons, who was to prove immensely powerful invincible for everyone, except lord Shiva, who was likely to be the sole person capable of slaying Jalandhar.

The boy was reared up by the ocean on the advice of the creator. He was married to a beautiful girl named Vrinda, the daughter of the demon Kalinemi, when Jalandhar came of age. Now, Jalandhar continued to become more and more powerful. The demon priest Shukracharya was quite pleased and appointed him as the demon-lord, Seeing Jalandhar's illimitable power, Shukracharya told Jalandhar as to how Vishnu, cunningly had reserved the nectar for gods and had this demon beheaded. Hearing this, Jalandhar sent a courier to the chief of gods Indra. She sought the divine chief to return the jewels recovered from the churning of ocean or face war. Indra treated his messenger with utter contempt and when he reported this matter to his lord, Jalandhar, the latter declared war on gods. Either sides had their number of causalities, but Shukracharya the demon preceptor, managed to revive the dead demons by the wonder drug, Sanjeevani that he had. The preceptor of gods, Brihaspati got hold of similar drug from the Mount Drona. Jalandhar was surprised to see even the gods though slain were relived to life. So, he asked his preceptor, Shukracharya: 'Acharya! How come that even the divine soldiers get back life when you alone had this power to accomplish?' The demon-preceptor replied: 'They are getting the wonder drug from the mount Drona.' He advised Jalandhar to uproot the mount so that the deceased gods might not be revived to life. demon preceptor did so, the gods started losing the battle, as he had thrown that mount into the sea. Since the situation became very critical for gods, on the advice of Brihaspati, Indra had to accept cease-fire. The gods lost and fled hellter skelter. Jalandhar established his hold without any trouble on the divine capital Amaravati.

The vanquished gods reassembled in a secret Himalayan care and brooded over their future course of action. They decided to seek help from lord Vishnu to retrieve their lost empire. Lord Vishnu was ready, as ever, to help gods. Lakshmi, lord Vishnu's consort heard about the gods scheme, she sought her lord not to kill Jalandhar, as he was her brother [both had their origin from water (ocean). Vishnu acceded to her request and befriended the demon, to the great chagrin of gods. The gods then sought the scheming sage Narad's advice who said: 'Not until this demon-lord antagonizes lord Shiva that he could be slain.' And on the gods' request, he devised a scheme and went to meet Jalandhara.

Jalandhara was delighted to have the divine sage, Narad, in his realm and offered her obeisance. Narad then told him: 'O demon lord! I'm coming straight from the realms of lord Shiva, which extends to more than 10,000 yojanas. You have everything best that the life can offer you: I was told that even your realm matches well with that realm while I roamed across. It was to confirm this contention that I came here in your realm. No doubt, you have everything that lord Shiva possesses, but you lack in one thing. Lord Shiva has a gem of woman as his consort, who is incomparable. You may also have your Realm not lacking in anything, if you could get hold of that gem of a woman.

Getting duped by Narad's sweet talks, the demon decided to take up cudgels against lord Shiva and dispatched his courier to the realm of lord Shiva with the express demand that Parvati, the consort of lord Shiva, be sent to his realm. Lord Shiva was furious to hear this outrageous demand. His anger produced a terrible being called Barbara, who went to Jalandhar and warned him of dire consequences, if the latter did not come and apologized before lord Shiva. Since Jalandhar's ego had been bloated by Narad, Jalandhar refused to apologise. On the contrary, he decided to attack lord Shiva with his full army. Soon, a fierce battle took place in which the demons had to flee before the terrible might of the henchmen of lord Shiva. Seeing his forces depleted, the demon decided to fight a war of illusion. He quickly disguised himself as lord Shiva and reached before Parvati to abduct her. But seeing the goddess's exquisite beauty, he ejaculated incontrollably and was thus exposed. Parvati then hid herself in a secret cave.

Lord Shiva heard about Jalandhar's heinous attempt, he consulted lord Vishnu, saying: 'Why are you still siding with this immoral demon? Why don't you come out and help gods?' Lord Vishnu told lord Shiva the reason behind his support to Jalandhar, who was in a way Lakshmi's brother. Lakshmi inquired him not to take cudgels against his brother-in-law. Lord Vishnu heard about Jalandhar's outrageous attempt to kidnap Parvati, he said: 'This demon is deriving all powers, because of his wife Vrinda's total devotion. Since, he has attempted to outrage the modesty of Parvati, you have every right to pay him in the same coin by making a similar attempt.'

And on lord Shiva's advice, lord Vishnu repaired to the realm of Jalandhar and stayed there in a garden. Meanwhile, the devoted wife of the demon lord Jalandhar, Vrinda, once dreamt that her husband, naked with oil smeared on his face and body was heeding southwards. He appeared clad in only a garland of black flowers and was surrounded with dreadful beasts. When she woke up, she was quite disturbed and in her attempt to shake off that dreadful vision, went to that garden with the company of her friends. She suddenly found the whole garden covered with dreadful beings. Her friends fled in panic and Vrinda, terrified, went near that ascetic under penance, who was none other than lord Vishnu in disguise. The ascetic let out a weird cry to shoo all the gods away and Vrinda, in her relief, put her hands round the neck of that ascetic. She espied two monkeys coming there with the head and the torso of Jalandhar, who was presumably dead, while she was with the ascetic. She sought the ascetic to relive her dead husband and the ascetic replied: 'No one, slain by lord Shiva's wrath could be brought back to life. Since you have sought my shelter, I would request Him to help me relive this body.'

He did so and Vrinda found her husband alive. Happily she surrendered herself to her husband's passion and they enjoyed for long.

But verily, her husband was not the real Jalandhar, but a clone or an illusive creation of lord Vishnu. Lord Vishnu, thus on the advice of lord Shiva, had violated her wifely devotion by making her surrender to the passion of illusive husband. This made her husband's power wane. Vrinda learnt about the deceit played on her, she cursed lord Vishnu: 'You shall also be separated from your wife who shall be abducted by a demon in the Treta Yuga.' Lord Vishnu sought her compassion, which made her modify the curse by saying that he will get back his abducted wife with the help of monkey brigade. Having said so, she immolated herself by the Holy Fire created out of her yoga sadhana. Her vital force entered the body of Parvati, so far hiding in a cave frightened of Jalandhar's amoral advances. She came out again in the open, to the great delight of her husband, lord Shiv, and of the gods when that vital force of Vrinda entered Parvati's body.

Getting his wife back, lord Shiva renewed his attack on Jalandhar, now considerably weakened because of his wife's demise. The demon raged a magic war, making an illusion as though lord Shiva's consort Parvati, appeared tied to his chariot's one wheel. Deeming her wife to be in that pathetic state, Lord Shiva assumed his dreadful Rudra form, and hacked off the demon-lord Jalandhar's body by his famous trident. The vital force that emerged from Jalandhar's body coalesce with the body of lord Shankara. The gods, delighted at being rid of the mighty enemy, sang in unison in praise of lord Shiva.

It is mentioned that Vrinda, in her next life, took birth as the sacred tulsi plant (basil) and her that personalized form was the darling of lord Krishna in Dwapara Age.

[The whole episode appears to be an extended allegory. It appears that this sacred plant was the preserve of water (Jalandhara) and the gods, realizing the special medicinal qualities of basil tried to make it grow on the land, where this could be put to better use. All the subsequent tales regarding Vrinda points to this logical conclusion. In fact, most of the Hindu Scriptures have scientific facts so thickly woven in the form of fictional tales that it becomes difficult to separate the chaff from the real grain. This whole episode is a classical example of that attempt.]

When Sanat Kumar concluded the tale, sage Vedvyasji said that verily Jalandhar was the fraction of lord Shankara himself. It was Lord Shiva's sportive play.

Lord Shankara then told gods that one should always be wary of *Maya* (illusive play) that is always God's creation to test the faith of devotees.

1. Ekadashi Fast and Modes of Worship

The assembled saints asked sage Vyasji that: 'Whether there is any sacred date (lunar tithi) on which one could observe fast and get the benefit of the fasts kept for the entire month?' Vyasji whereupon told them that Ekadashi of the both fortnights (bright as well as the dark) is one such date. If anyone keeps fast on this day, one gets merit for the entire month. On every Ekadashi date, man should keep fast and pray the date this way. 'O Ekadashi! Give me strength to remain devoted to lord Vishnu. This is the most favourite date of lord Vishnu.

The sages then asked the various modes of worship in the different months and Vyasji obliged by enlightening then the mode of worship on for every month in the year. The details are given below:

(i)   **Caitra Month:** During this month, the fragrant flowers should be soaked overnight in pure water and the idol of the lord should be bathed in that water. The worship should be done by lighting incense, offering water-mixed milk and flowers. The flowers should be Bilwa (wood apple tree's) and of the lotus plant.

(ii)   **Vaisakha Month:** During this month, the deity's worship must include the offering made with the flower of Ketaki. The deity's idol should be bathed in curds apart from the other ritual items as mentioned in the previous lunar month. Very light clothes should be worn.

(iii) **Jyeshtha Month:** The devotees should bathe in cold water and offer the fruits of Anwala to the deity. During the worship, the deity's idol should be vigorously fanned to create fresh wind draughts. A garland of patal fruits should be offered. The prasadam should be made of sattu flour mixed in sugar and cold water. [Sattu flour is made from barley].

(iv) **Ashadh Month:** Having bathed the idol of the lord in curds it should be offered the garland of Kadamb flower. The fan should be made of peacock feathers for creating fresh air. The garland could be made of Ketaki and Harshigar flowers. For bhog or prasad fresh butter should used. [During the months of Vaishakha, Jyeshtha and Ashadh, only very light clothes should be used for covering the deity's idol.

(v)   **Shravan Month:** The deity should be bathed in a fragrant water and the flowers offered should be of 'Mauli-shree' and Kadamba. For prasadam, lightly roasted in ghee, fresh rice grains (or Kheelam) should be used.

(vi) **Bhadrapada Month:** In the beginning of this month, lord Narayana's idol should be installed in a new temple, which should be liberally incensed. During the night, the idol-deity should be covered in a mosquito net. During this month, Ketaki flowers should not be used in worship.

Lord Narayana should be worshipped with fresh flower, offering preferably those grown in a pond. During this month, the devotees must not eat food after the sunset,

(vii) **Ashwin Month:** During this entire month, the deity's idol should be bathed only in fresh water. The bathing ceremony should be held before noon as after the sun reaching mid-heaven, the deity would deem this water as blood and hence unacceptable. Hence, the ceremonies should be held before moonrise.

(viii) **Kartika Month:** This is held as the most pious month and the devotee should shun from having meat, indulging in intercourse with wife. His eatables shouldn't be cooked in oil. The devotee must be very cautious about personal hygiene as well. During the night, the *Deepa-Daan* ceremony must be held with full rituals. In Kartik, the worship must include offering of the bilwa patra. It is believed that alms given during this month give tremendous merit to devotees. The flowers used for worship must be white in colour or generally of light-shade.

(ix) **Margshirsha Month:** During this month, lord Vishnu should be worshipped with his consort Lakshmi. Singing devotional songs with total concentration brings good reward during this month. The prasadam offered to the deity must include ripe oranges. In general, offering fresh fruits for prasadam should be religiously adhered to.

(x) **Pausha Month:** In this month (lunar) Pausha, lord Krishna should be worshipped because He is the manifestation of lord Vishnu only. The prasadam offered should be sugarcane juice and sugar cane. The idols of the deity should be clad in warm clothes and the devotional music must be accompanied by musical instruments.

(xi) **Magha Month:** Following the completion of the pancha yajna, the deity should be worshipped after bathing the idol in warm water. The idol's body should be annointed with a thin solution of sandalwood paste and water. The deity should be worshipped with the offering of champa flowers.

(xii) **Phalguna Month:** During this month, the deity should be worshipped with genda (marigold) flowers and the prasadam should be of *thandayee*. The body of the idol should be bathed in luke warm water.

Telling thus sage Vyasji said: 'Now, I have told you all how the deity should be worshipped in twelve months of the year. Remember, however, that worship of the deity has primary condition of purity of feeling. Even if you falter in the method and form of worshipping, the deity would not mind if you are genuine in the feeling. Lord Narayana remains happy with the devotee, who has a guileless heart and pristine feeling devotion. Lord Narayana controls the riches and wealth of this entire world through this consort Lakshmi. As such, Lord Narayana has no influence of the devotee showering riches in the worship. He who wants to influence the deity controlling all wealth through his ostentatious display of wealth is verily an idiot.'

At the end of each worship, the devotee should pray this way: 'O Lord Narayana! I am an ignorant person and know nothing about the form or rituals. I have only a feelingful heart. So, God, please forgive me if I have committed any mistake in form. I crave for nothing else, but your grace. Please grant me.'

2. The Importance of Taking Bath

Now the sages asked Vyasji as to how much importance was accorded to bathing during different months.

Starting with the narration, Vyasji told the sages: 'O sages! I tell you this importance as related to Dashrath by Vasishtha, Dattatreya to Kartaveerya and Brahma to Narada. Narada had related it to Sahastrabahu. The gist of the same I relate to you all.'

In our country, due to tropological condition, bathing has great significance. It not only ensures one's piety, but also keeps aspirant free from diseases. However, having bath in the early morning during the entire month of Magh has great significance. He who is bornin Aryavarta and doesn't take bath in the month of Magh gets next life as a goat. He wastes his life like the glands handing down from a goat's neck. All his pious deeds will become rather unmeritorious, if he doesn't take bath in the month of Magh early in the morning everyday. He who takes bath everyday in the month of Magh (Dec-Jan.) remains free of diseases for the entire year. One should bathe before the sunrise. Narrating an episode by the advantages or benefits of having early bath during the month of Magha, Vyasji recounted a story which is given below.

In very olden times, there was a pious brahmin woman in the lineage of Bhrigu, whose name was Kubjika. She became widow when young. Getting unhappy with her life, she started dwelling on the banks of the river Narmada. Every day early in the morning, before sunrise, she would go through her cleansing rituals and take bath in the river Narmada at the day break. She bathed for sixty years and never missed her bathing ritual during the month of Magh. With the result, after death she went to lord Vishnu's realm where she dwelt for a one full cycle of the four ages. Then after by the grace of her maintaining piety, Brahma made her absolutely beautiful. She was reborn as Tilottama—a lady with a faultless organs and body. Brahma had sent her to the earth for destroying the demons. While she was on the earth the too powerful demon brothers, Sunda and Upasanda, fell for her and fought against each other to have her as their wife. Eventually in their lust for her, they killed each other and helped thus the divine cause of eliminating the demonic influence from the earth.

Further emphasising on the necessity of taking bath particularly during the month of Magh. Vyasji said: 'Persons of all caste and category are entitled to have bath during the month of Magh. This kind of ritual bath cleanses one of all impurities and destroys one's sins.'

He further said that taking bath during the month of Kartika and giving alms ensures one's nook in the realm of Vishnu. Delving on the details, the sage said that one should defecate during this month facing north and keeping the sacred thread (Yagyopavitra or Janevu) above one's night ear. After cleansing ritual, one should offer alms to the poor brahmins every morning in the month of Kartika. Some of the things forsaken during this month: cereal from other's house, use of other's bed, meeting other's women, non-vegetarian food, til (sesame seeds), buffalo or the goats' milk etc. On the 14th lunar (bright) day of the month of Kartika, one should keep fast. On the Ekadashi day of this month, the ritual marriage of tulsi (plant) with lord Krishna should be celebrated with much fanfare in the background of devotional music.

There are different names to the baths taken in during the month of Kartika. They are tested as below.

(i) **Varuna Snaana:** This the type of bathing perform in dipping one's body in the water of a river, pond, or ocean.

(ii) **Vaayavya Snaana:** Rubbing the dust taken from the feet of a cow over one's entire body is called Vaayavya Snaana.

(iii) **Divya Snaana.** Taking bath in the rain water is called Divya Snana.

(iv) **Brahma-Snana:** Taking bath in the well-water, while chanting mantras is called Brahma Snana.

Among these, the best snana (bath) is the one called Vaaruna Snana which gives most merit. Whole taking bath persons of all categories: Brahmana, Kshatriya, Vaishya should chant holy mantras. The Shoodras must take bath in total silence.

While quoting lord Krishna, Vedavyas recounted a story of Dhaneshwar. Dhaneshwar was a perverted Brahmin, who was very wicked. Once while searching for his target to cheat people, he happened to reach Mahishmati city. The holy men were observing Kartika Vrata. Since all were busy, he had no go, but to wait. He kept on listening to the holy mantras and kept waiting for the persons to come to the ground from the river Narmada. Meanwhile, he was bitten by a deadly snake. Dhaneshwara found dead when they assembled there, they put some leaves of tulsi and holy water down his throat. Soon, he expired and his soul was taken away by the couriers of Yama. Since, he had no good deed to his credit, he was consigned to Kumbhi-Paak hell. The atmosphere became very quiet and holy, to the great surprise of its guards when he reached there. They reported the matter to lord Yama, who sought Narada's opinion on this queer case. Narada searched through his records and found that since he had died at a holy spot, his sins were destroyed. Eventually he became entitled to staying in heaven.

Such is the glory of having bath every day. [In fact, curiously enough, all the holy baths are prescribed by the

Scriptures mostly in winter season (like the month of Magh or Kartika. It appears the purpose behind such instruction is medical though they get covered in the sheen of the religious dictates. This has been the general trend as we have already pointed before].

3. Avataars of lord Vishnu

Vyasji told the sages that lord Vishnu's each *avataar* was for a specific purpose.

(i) Matsyaavataar [Fish Incarnation]

Matsyavataar was the first incarnation of lord Vishnu. It occurred to redeem the earth and life from the onslaught of water.

When the process of creation commenced, Brahma first created the nine Prajapatis (progenitors) viz., Bhrigu, Atri, Maruchi, Daksha, Kardam, Pulastya, Pulaha, Angira and Kratu, who helped Him in the process of creation. From Maruchi was born Kashyapa. Kashyapa had four wives: Aditi, Diti, Kadru and Vinata. These four wives created respectively the gods (from Aditi), the demons (from Diti), the snakes (from Kadru) and the birds including Garuda (from Vinata).

After sometime, the progeny of Diti, the demons overpowered. Brahma had to snatch the holy Vedas from his possession. Having snatched the Vedas, the prominent demons namely Shambuka, Hayagreeva, Hiranyakashyapa, Mahabala and Hiranyaksha entered shallow deep the ocean. It appeared as though the whole knowledge was lost. The gods then requested lord Vishnu to rescue knowledge. Lord Vishnu adopted the form of a behemoth fish and entered ocean's abyss to retrieve the core of knowledge. He had a duel with a demon called Makar, who hid the Vedas in the ocean. The lord defeated the demons and reorganized Vedas to restore knowledge back on planet earth. [It is an allegorical explanation. In fact after the Grand Dissolution or Maha Pralaya when the entire universe appeared inundated with water, even life was facing extinction. In order to wade through water and preserve life, lord Vishnu assumed the convenient form of a behemoth fish to rescue life and knowledge that existed before the Pralaya. This kind of Pralaya is described in every civilization in the world. The 'Nooha ki Kishti' or 'Noah's Arc of respectively Muslims and Christians indicate the similar situation] It is believed that later on lord Vishnu appeared as Vedavyas to re-edit and vet the entire knowledge represented by the Vedas.

(ii) Koormavatar [Tortoise Incarnation]

Telling about this second incarnation of lord Vishnu, Vyasji quoted the dialogue between lord Shiv and Parvati to say that long ago, once sage Durvasa went to meet the divine chief, Indra. He saw Indra getting adored by fellow-gods and was feeling elated. In his happiness, sage Durvasa gave Indra a garland of lotus flower. But Indra, contemptuously put that garland around the neck of his mount, elephant Eiravat. But, as Indra left for Nandanvana, the pachyderm threw that garland on the land and trod under its heavy foot. Sage Durvasa could see this insult meted out to his gift. He became so charged that he cursed Indra that the divine chief would soon lose all his pelf and prosperity. As he cursed the divine chief Indra's Amaravati lost its glory. The gods lost their power and position. They became increasingly lack-lustre. Severely distressed the gods sought shelter of lord Vishnu for relief. At last, Vishnu appeared before them and advised gods to churn the ocean to retrieve gems. 'Only the gems churned out of the sea will be able to give them back prosperity, symbolized by Lakshmi, who had entered the ocean following sage Durvasa's curse from heaven to the ocean. The gods found themselves incapable of doing alone and on lord Vishnu's advice, they sought help from the demons as well. The two groups used Vasuki as the churning rope and Mandarachal as the churner. But, the problem arose as the mount Mandarachal, being used as the churner, couldn't float on the sea water. It needed a base to stand upon. At last, lord Vishnu assumed the form of a gigantic tortoise (Koorma) to stabilize the mount. So, lord Vishnu's second incarnation as Koorma took place to help the gods retrieve lost treasure from the ocean. After the churning, Lakshmi reappeared on the earth and espoused lord Vishnu. Indra realized his mistake of insulting a great sage and Lakshmi reappeared to be praised her profusely. In this manner, lord Vishnu helped gods again to restore their glory by appearing as the tortoise.

(iii) Varaha Avataar [Boar-Incarnation]

Lord Vishnu's third incarnation was in the form of a boar. Telling this story, lord Shankara had informed Parvati that there were two guards named Jaya and Vijaya in the realm of lord Vishnu. Once they prevented the child sage Sanat-Kumar from entering lord Vishnu's realm. This made Sanat Kumar curse them to become demons. In the next life, both of them had appeared as the demon-lords Hiranyaksha and Hiranyakashyapa. The demon duo were brothers. Hiranyaksha had become so powerful that he established his rule over the entire earth, to swipe from the divine hold. He uprooted the entire earth along with life and placed shallow the ocean. Then at the gods' request, lord Vishnu again appeared as giagantic boar with two horns on his head. This boar entered shallow deep into the ocean and killed Hiranyaksha with his one horn and rescued earth from other horn. He brought out the earth from the ocean and placed it on its even keel.

[Again this is an allegory. We all know that a boar is the

best scavenger among the animals. After the Pralaya, when the earth started to emerge out from water, it was fully covered with slush and filth. In order to clean its filth, lord Vishnu appeared as the gigantic boar to make it sprout life again].

(iv) Nrisimha Avataar (Man-Lion Incarnation)

Among the incarnations of lord Vishnu, the Man-Lion or Nrisimha incarnation has special significance. [It also shows the transition or evolution of life from plainly aquatic beings to other species-like man or lion. This stage shows the transition phase of life from the beast to human form].

Following the slaying of his brother Hiranyaksha at the hands of lord Vishnu, Hiranyakashyapa was greatly annoyed. He wanted to avenge his brother's death at the hands of lord Vishnu. He performed a rigorous penance to propitiate lord Brahma with this intention. Lord Brahma appeared before him and he asked the boon of immorality. However, lord Brahma refused, saying those born in this mortal world must die. The demon then sought the following boon: 'There should be no death by man or beast, or in the air or sky, or during day or night or inside or outside the house.' He demanded the boon almost ensuring immorality. The creator said, 'So, be it', yet the demon didn't know how the divinity could circumvent those conditions.

The demon, after receiving the boon became very mighty and ruled over the earth. He promulgated the order that all the yajnas for granting strength to the gods be stopped forthwith and they should worship him instead of any god particularly lord Vishnu. While panic reigned the entire world, the sole defiant to this rule was none else but Hiranyakashyapa's own son, Prahlad, who became an arch devotee of lord Vishnu. His father learnt about his defiance and made efforts to force his son not worship lord Vishnu. He even tried to have his son murdered by all possible means but each time the boy Prahlad survived. At last, the demon chief, Hiranyakashyapa himself came to murder with his mace. But, Prahlad would not listen, he kept on saying that lord Vishnu existed in every bit of creation. 'He is in every thing, in me, in you, in everything that we see around and across.' Hiranyakashyapa whereupon said: 'Is he also in this pillar to which you are bound.' 'Yes' asserted Prahlad. The demon chief thenhurled a massive blow on to the pillar Prahlad was tied to. As this made struck the pillar, with a lound thunder, the pillar came asunder and emerged from it a queer figure: a huge man with the head of a lion. With a stentorian laughter, he lifted Hiranyakashyapa and put him on to his lap and with his bare claws, he tore the demon apart. Hiranyakashyapa was killed during the dusk, which was neither day nor night, in the lap of that huge being neither in the air nor sky, at the threshold of the main entrance, which was neither inside nor outside the house. Thus fulfilling all conditions, that huge man-beast, called Nrisimha, an incarnation of lord Vishnu killed that demon lord, while Prahlad kept chanting his prayers to lord Vishnu. This was the fourth incarnation of lord Vishnu. To save gods and protect his arch devotee, Prahlad, lord Vishnu thereby eliminated the evil forces represented by the demon lord, Hiranyakashyapa.

(v) Vaamana Avataar [Dwarf Incarnation]

This was the fifth incarnation of lord Vishnu. [By the time, this incarnation took place, the evolution to the stage of man proper was complete and hence lord Vishnu appeared as a full-fledged human being].

Raja Bali was the desendant of the family of Hiranyakashyapa, his son was Prahalad, whose son was Virochas and Virochan's son was Raja Bali. Raja Bali, unlike most demon-lords was a religious person and had total control over his senses. He was renowned for charity. He was, at the same time, quite powerful and had won the realms including that ruled by gods. In order to defeat him, the gods hatched a conspiracy. Seeing them totally helpless and forlorn, they went to lord Vishnu and besought to get back their lost glory. The gods requested the divine-sire Kashyapa to ask lord Vishnu to find a means to outwit Raja Bali. Lord Vishnu decided to adopt the form of a Brahmin-lad, a batuk, who was very short. He then went to the yajna, being performed by Raja Bali. Since, Raja Bali was renowned for title not letting any medicant go from his door empty handed. Lord Vishnu decided to exploit this quality of Raja Bali.

Adopting an adolescent but dwarf Brahmin son's form, called Vamana (since his height is said to be only 52 'angula' or finger's breadth and '52' in Sanskrit called Vamana), he reached the venue of the yajna, where Raja Bali was doling alms out to the medicants. As he (lord Vishnu) reached there and was about to have his demand fulfilled by Raja Bali, the demon-preceptor, Shukracharya, detected lord Vishnu in that Vamana form and asked his king Bali to think before he granted the desire of that Brahmin boy. However, the king was adamant. He told Shukracharya in whispers: 'If lord Vishnu has come to his door as a mandicant, I won't let him go empty handed. On the contrary, I will feel honoured to have fulfilled the desire of the Super-God.'

Shukracharya was still not quiet. He adopted a tiny form and entered the water-pot's snout through which the water came out. As Raja Bali asked Vamana to have his desire fulfilled and wanted to take votive water into his palm, water from that pot didn't come out. Lord Vishnu then in Vamana form pierced a sharp edged grass into that spout which damaged Shukracharya's one eye. Eventually, water came out. Vamana had demanded that he might own the land his three steps could measure. Raja Bali said: 'So, be it.' As the king gave his word, Vamana (lord Vishnu in disguise) began to grow bigger and bigger. Soon, he became as big as almost to scrape the sky. In his one step, he measured the entire earth in the next the heavenly realm. Now, he asked Raja Bali as to where should he put his third step. Raja Bali whereupon offered his head and lord Vishnu put his feet upon Raja Bali's head to push him down to the nether world (Patal-Loka). This delighted at having made heaven and earth out of Raja Bali's ready lord Vishnu told him: 'You may rule Patal Loka and away for one month in a year you will be able to come on to the earth. [Onam festival in Kerala is celebrated to herald Raja Bali's annual visit to the earth]. This way, lord Vishnu in his Vamana incarnation get rid of Bali and protected the divine interest and restored the gods lost glory.

(vi) **Parashuram's Avataar (Incarnation of Ram with Axe)**
This incarnation of lord Vishnu had taken place to subdue the reckless and delinquent Kshatriyas, who were becoming totally egoistic and uncontrollable.

The story goes like it. Once sage Jamadagni had pleased Indra as much as to get the divine cow, Surabhi, from him. After some time, the famous king Kaartaveerya happened to visit sage Jamadagni's hermitage with his entire entourage. The sage treated him and his group very lavishly. When the sage how he could treat them so lavishly, the sage said that it was on account of the divine cow that he possessed. The king whereupon asked him to gift his cow to him. The sage bluntly refused. The king then forcibly took possession of the cow and left. The king found the cow on his way growing uncontrollably violent. She injured most of his soldiers by her horns and kicks, not even sparing the king. The king also bit the sage and wounded him in anger. He then went away with the cow triumphantly.

Parashuram was Jamdagni's son. He heard about Raja

Kaartaveerya wounding his father, after having honed his famous axe be went to settle scores with the Raja, who was said to have a thousand arms and was also known as Sahastraarjuna. Parashuram not only killed this king, but taught lessons to various such insolent Kshatriya king as many as twenty one times. Having rid the earth of reckless violence, lord Vishnu in his sixth incarnation restored the rule of propriety on the earth.

(vii) Lord Ram's Avataar [The Ram Incarnation].

Vishnu incarnated as lord Ram in order to establish the ideal rule over earth. Lord Ram showed how an ideal son should behave and how an ideal king should rule. Since, he established the *Maryada* (norms of propriety), he is frequently referred to as *Maryada Purushottam* (*Man Par-Excellence*).

It may be recalled that when Sanata Kumar the child sage cursed Jaya-Vijaya, the guard of Vishnu's realm to become demon, the curse was to continue for more than one life. They become Hiranyaksha and Hiranyakashyapa while in the next life and they were born as Ravan and Kumbhakarna in their subsequent life. They were the sons of Vichirawa who was sage Pulastya's son. Vichirawa had a wife Kaikesi from the demon-clan. He had three sons and a daughter from him. They were Ravana, Kumbhakarna, Vibhishana and the girl Soorpanakha. Since alone Vibhishana was born out of Vichirawa and Kaikesi's union on a far day, alone he was endowed with noble qualities.

Ravana and Kumbhakarna performed very rigorous penance to cover the boon of unslayability by gods and of six months unbroken sleep in a year respectively. Having derived these boons, they began to live recklessly. Soon Ravana established his control over all the realms. Ravana was an ardent devotee of lord Shiva [Incidently, this incarnation of lord Vishnu as Ram is marked by the sharp divisive forces in the Sanatan Dharma (Hindu Dharma) emerging for claiming the supremacy between lord Shiva and lord Shankara, which continued upto Goswami Tulsidas's time. This saint poet had done a lot to remove the differences between the Shaivites and Vishnavites.] Troubled by Ravana and his demons, the gods requested lord Vishnu again to come to their rescue and liquidate Ravana. Lord Vishnu promised them that soon he would appear as the repriever of Raja Dashrath and Kausalya in Awadh. At due time, he appeared as lord Ram. [The saga of lord Rama is well known to be recounted for.] Lord Vishnu eventually killed Ravana and redeemed the earth from the evil forces. Through Ram's incarnation, lord Vishnu displayed an ideal in all human relationship as well as in administering of a state. Hence, he is called *Maryada Purushottam.*

(viii) Krishnavataar [Incarnation As Lord Krishna]

In this age, the sentinels of lord Vishnu's realm, Jaya-Vijaya, under the curse of the child sage Sanat-Kumar had been born as the tyrannical rulers Kamsa and Jarasandha. But essentially, lord Vishnu's incarnation was for acquainting people at large the difference between what is right and what is wrong or between righteousness [Dharma] and non-righteousness [Adharma]. In this incarnation, the lord had himself clarified that whenever there is decline of righteousness with the rise of non-righteousness, He decides to carnate.

When Kamsa, Jarasandha and other despotic rulers had troubled the earth, it sought lord Vishnu's shelter who assured her that soon he would appear on the earth as the son of Devaki and Vasudeva alongwith His all-powers to rid the earth of the tyranny. He was born when Devaki and Vasudeva were imprisoned in a jail by Kamsa. He inspired Vasudeva through His divine power that for His

(Krishna's) safety, Hewould be taken across the Yamuna in Nanda and Yashodha's house. He was reared up there by guardian Nanda and Yashoda. Although Kamsa made continuous attempt to kill him, he did not succeed. Not only Krishna and his elder brother, Balaram slayed many demons, they eventually managed to kill Kamsa. Subsequently, Krishna played the most significant role in *Mahabharat* and made the Pandavas (the lobby of the righteous) slay their unrighteous cousins, Kauravas and his support including Jarasandha-Krishna didn't mind employing even ulterior tricks to ensure achievement of the righteous and even through unrighteous means. In the end, when his own clan, the Yadavas behaved in an iniquitous manner, he helped their extiction as well. He would ever run off from the battlefield, if he found his continued fighting would cause much damage to the common people. He had shifted from Mathura to his newly established capital Dwarika to save the people of Mathura from Jarasandha's continued onslaughts.

In order to clarify the subtle distinction between what is righteous and what is unrighteous, he had used Arjun to give vent to His thoughts through his famous *Bhagavadgita*.

This incarnation of Krishna needed more potency to destroy the evil. During lord Ram's time, all evil was confined to Lanka. Lord Ram went there and eliminated it. But Krishna had more difficult task at hand, since by his time the evil had mixed so deeply with good that even one family had good and bad people. He had to sift them minutely to eliminate the evil. Hence, Krishna's incarnation had been the most potent incarnation of lord Vishnu thus far:

[Curiously enough, this Purana doesn't say anything about the ninth incarnation Gautam Buddha and the tenth incarnation, the future *Kulki* avataar.]

Following this description of the purpose behind, lord Vishnu's each incarnation, the sages expressed their desire to know about heaven, sub-heavens and the ways and means to achieve them. They asked the great sage to reveal about the fundamental truth of life, which is detailed by lord Krishna in his famous discourse renowned as *Srimad Bhagwatgita*. Lord Krishna himself says that this discourse contains the essence of life. About this, once Lakshmiji had asked lord Vishnu (or Krishna), one very irreverent question. 'Lord! I find you always lying on the snake coach in the Kheera Sagar. When do you perform your duty as the sustainer of the world?'

Smiling lord Vishnu, replied: 'Dear! I keep montoring the entire world every second. I have already given details to the world as to how should one keep an ideal life in every state of existene through my *Srimad Bhagwadgita*, which I made my incarnation Krishna say in the celebrated tome created by the most erudite sage of the world, Vedavyas. The people of the world know what they should do and I monitor what they are actually doing. I keep a close eye over all activities of the world and adopt measures to sustain it in this manner.'

Goddess Lakshmi whereupon asked about the importance and the essential message each canto of the *Shrimad Bhagavadgita* and lord Vishnu gave the brief analysis about them.

4. Srimad Bhagwadgita Cantos

(i) **First Canto:** This canto highlights the means through which a being can gain redemption from one's sins. There is a strong ground about it which says that a certain Brahmin named Susharma had been consigned to hell following his committing sins. There he had to undergo torture and eventually he was reborn as a lame bull. Owing to his being lame, nobody kept him at his place. The bull suffered an incurable disease and writhed in great pain. Seeing the bull's pitiable condition, a prostitute parted with part of her merits, which made him leave his mortal coil and get salvation.

(ii) **Second Canto:** In this chapter, the means are given through which one can graduate to higher species in the next life. There is a story attached with this chapter which is as follows. There was a very religious Brahman named Deva Sharma who was visiting south. There he met a realized sage, who enlightened Deva Sharma on the knowledge of self. He also recounted an episode that dwelling upon the banks of the river Godavari was a Brahmin named Durdan. He dwelled in the state ruled by king Vikram. But that Brahmin only cared for filling his own belly and for nothing else. Due to his this selfish outlook, he had to suffer much torture in hell. In the next life, he was born in a very lowly family and was married to a girl of the family of the same status. That girl was rather of loose character and enjoyed the company of other beings she happened to come in contact with a pariah (chandal) and from this union delivered a daughter, who became a Daakini (a kind of demoness) habitual to devour people. Subsequently, she got birth as a goat. That goat happened to come to me (Sage Vyas), who I reared up very lovingly. Later on, I saw a tiger seeing whom I fled in panic but the same beast came and stood near that goat, who remained undaunted. The goat offer the beast himself as food, but the beast said that of late he had become very Satvik (noble and kind hearted). He didn't know what turned so noble. Although, the goat and the tiger had no idea what brought about this change, yet an ape perched on a tree nearly knew this secret. The ape said that due to the beast's inadvertent listening to the second canto of the Gita he had become so non-violent. Thus due to listening that part of the Gita even, the beast got these noble feelings.

(iii) **Third Canto:** This part of the Gita is particularly good for redeeming the distressed manes. Telling a concerned story, Shivji (Lord Shiva) said that in the olden times a Brahmin forsook his brahminic pursuits and adopted the trait of doing trade and business. He had also started in indulging in gambling. Whatever he earned, he began to waste in wrong pursuits. Once when returning from abroad he was bringing a lot of wealth, but the same was looted by the dacoits who also eventually killed him. Owing to his wrong deeds in the next life he was born in a ghostly species. Meanwhile, this brahmin's son was a very noble person. He waited for long for his father's return, but later on when he enquired he learnt about these unfortunate circumstances in which his father had died. He expressed the desire of going to Kashi and doing the obsequies for his departed father. When going to Kashi, he stopped near the tree under which his father was killed. As he completed his routine of going through the third chapter of the Gita, he had a glimpse of his father in terrible form and subsequently in a tiny barley form. He saw his father coming down on a divine vehicle from the realm of lord Vishnu. He offered obeisance to his father. His father blessed him and told he need not go to Kashi anymore, because his reading the third canto of the Gita had accomplished his purpose.

(iv) **Fourth Canto:** This fourth canto enshrines methods for getting redemption from the travails of lives. Telling about its significance, lord Shankara said that once on the bank of river Ganga in Varanasi, there lived an ascetic named Bharat. Everyday, he used to study the fourth canto of the Gita. One day the same Mahatma went for a walk. He used to study this canto everyday near the bush of *Jhambeni plumes*. Having followed his routine he went for a walk. Owing to the effect of his that study two trees near the Jharbari plumes bushes got another life as two daughters in that brahmin's house. After seven years of their birth when both daughters saw that peripatetic sage, they expressed their gratitude for having helped them get better species in this life.

(v) **Fifth Canto:** This canto tells how a man can keep himself purified and pious. Telling this importance of canto, lord Shankara told Parvati that in olden times in Madra Pradesh, there dwelled a brahmin. But forsaking his routine of studying the Vedas, he had acquired much expertise in dancing and singing. He got entry into the royal court with his expertise, . He became quite delinquent when he got monetary awards. He managed to marry a danseuse called Aruna with the lure of the money. However, that danseuse was quite independent minded and she didn't like the constraints her husband had created for her. So, one day seizing his opportunity and managed to murder her husband. She expired after undergoing much torture due to her misdeeds. Brahmin Pingala became a hawk in the subsequent life, as a consequence of previous deeds, but Aruna a she-parrot. When the hawk identified the she-parrot, owing to previous birth's ill-will it came swifting at the she-parrot and instantly killed it. That hawk was also killed by a leopard. Tthe death-god Yama decided to grant them the higher species on reaching his realm. For, they had fallen in a human skull filled with water during their fight. This skull belonged to an ascetic dwelling on the banks of the river Ganga, who quit his mortal coil while chanting the fifth canto of the Gita. That merit was still potent which relieved both Pingala and Aruna from worldly travails.

(vi) **Sixth Canto:** The reading of this canto ensures one the merit one deserves after performing great yajnas which grant salvation. Telling the related story, lord Shankara recounted a story to Parvati. There dwelled a very religious -minded and noble king on the banks of the river Godavari His name was Jana-shruti. Propitiated with alms giving and performing yajnas, the gods from heaven descended in his state in the form of swans and asked him to have his boons They found the king emitting a divine light illuminating the path, while moving through the aried way. The swan whereupon said that his emitted light appeared brighter than that emitted by Mahatma Rikva. The king sent his charioteer along with his chariot to respectfully bring the sage Rikva to his kingdom. Passing through many pilgrimage centres that charioteer reached Kashmir and sought the sage to accompany. Rikva said he had no desire left, but should anyone want he could help him fulfil his desires. The charioteers returned without the sage and conveyed the sage's answer that he had all his desires satiated and should the king want, be should come to him. The king went to the sage Rikva after filling his chariot with expensive gems. The sage lost his temperament on noticing the wealth saying: 'Why have you brought these gems? The king quickly held the sage's feet in apology and said how he could become so indifferent to material riches. The sage replied: 'This is due to my reading the six the canto of the Gita, which ensures redemption from desires' The king then made it a routine to read the sixth canto of Gita every day.

(vii) **Seventh Canto:** This canto ensures better condition for human beings. Telling a story to highlight this canto's significance, lord Shankara told Parvati that there was a Brahmin in Pataliputra called Shankukaran, who earned much wealth by becoming a trader, but never cared for departed ancestors or for offering anything to the divinities. He had married thrice already and when he was going to marry for the fourth time, he died of snake bite, as there was no possible treatment. His next birth was in the species of the snakes. He had great infatuation for money that made him guard his wealth accrued to him in his previous life. Once he gave a dream to his sons in the previous life, telling about his stored wealth. On the next day, his one son was digging the earth to unearth the treasure that snake told him about his portable condition and asked his son to chant the seventh canto of Gita so that he might get better state. The son made his all brothers religiously chant the seventh canto of Gita and ultimately Shankar-Karan was redeemed from his potiable state.

(viii) **Eighth Canto:** The reading or chant of this canto not only grants one much knowledge and wisdom, but also ensures a better species in the next life. Telling a story, lord Shankara told Parvati that there was a wicked person named Bhava Sharma. Despite his being a Brahmin, he ate meat, drank liquor and indulged in looting and cheating others. One day owing to his heavy drinking bouts, he died. In the next life, he became a palm tree. In that very city, there also dwelled a Brahmin called Khushibal, who with his wicked wife used to usurp other's property. After death, both became *Brahma Rakshasa* (a deadly ghost category) and began to dwell under the shade of that very palm tree. One day, his wife asked as to how could they get relief from the present state of affairs, and the brahmin's answer was only getting an enlightening spiritual lesson. His wife asked whereupon how could it be possible. At that very moment, his memory of the previous birth got revived and began chanting the eighth canto of the Gita by rote. The couple got instant redemption from that deadly condition even when he could utter only half a shloka. Bhara Sharma, even now a palm-tree also got redemption from entering that shloka. The Brahmin made his routine since then to chant that canto from the Srimad Bhagavadgita every day.

(ix) **Ninth Canto:** The chanting or reading of the ninth canto of the Gitra ensures one's physical and astral comforts and redemption from such troubles. Lord Shiva told Parvati about the related story that there lived a person named Madhava on the banks of river Narmada in the city of Mahishmati. Once he organized a huge yajna in which a goat was to be sacrificed. Before the sacrifice, the goat was being bathed, it suddenly started laughing and said in a contemptuous tone: 'What advantage of such yajnas which are based on animal sacrifice.' The poor animal loses its life while the doer may get heaven and wealth. The priests asked the goat as to who he actually was when they heard him speaking so. The goat said: 'I was a Brahmin of a noble lineage in my previous life. My wife, desirous of having a son from me, requested me to arrange a goat for sacrificing at the altar of Mother Goddess Durga. That goat's mother cursed me to become a goat in my next life when I arranged to kill the goat.' The goat then said that there was one more related incident. Once on the occasion of the solar eclipse, a king called Chandra Sharma donated an idol of Kaal Purush to his priest. Some dark tiny being emerged from the heart region of that Kaal Purush and began to attack the priest and other Brahmin. No sooner the priest, out of his sheer habit, began to recite the ninth canto of the Gita, all those evil forces ran away and peace was restored quickly.' The chanting of the ninth canto thus ensures speedy recovery from physical and astral troubles.

(x) **Tenth Canto:** Lord Shankara told Parvati that there dwelled a Dheera Buddhi named Brahmin in the town of Kashipur. He was so devoted to me to lord Shankara that whenever he moved the lord himself guided his way holding his hand. Once lord Shankara's hench person asked the reason behind his showing much of consideration to that Brahmin. 'I told him', said lord Shankara, 'that he had accomplished many mentorious deeds. Once, I sat at my place over the mount Kailash, when a huge storm developed to disturb everything. The sky became pitched dark. Suddenly, a dark shaded bird then alighted from the sky and offering lotus to my feet with awe praised me in reverence. He replied that he was the swan of lord Brahma when I asked him who he was. I suddenly fell down while flying over the lotus filled pond. My colour as such has become so dark.' A lotus-bud replied about the reason of its turning black that she was a very beautiful Brahmin girl in the previous life, and has always served her master (husband) well. One day her playing with a Mynah made her indifferent to her husband, who cursed her to become a Mynah herself. 'When I died', the bird informed, 'I became a Mynah in my next life. But the sage's girl who reared me up was very particular of reading the tenth canto every day. Listening to her recital I became an Apsara named Padmavati in my subsequent life.'

(xi) **Eleventh Canto:** In the rewards for reading this eleventh canto, there is no provision of getting salvation. The related story is as follows.

Long ago, there was a very affluent city prospering on

the banks of the river Praneeta. There dwelled in that city called Medhankar, a devoted Vishmita named Sunanda. Everyday he would recite the eleventh canto of Gita religiously. He happened to go on pilgrimage with some friends while doing so. He happened to reach near a city called Vivaha-Mandap while roaming across. The head of the city administration allowed him to stay in the Dharmashala. Sunanda was amazed to find his friends missing in the subsequent morning while the dwellers of that queen city were bewildered to find her still alive and kicking. Some days after the head-man of the city made his son's friend stay in that Dharmashala alongwith his son as well. Next day, the city head-man found his son also becoming the food of a demon. He came to the Brahmin weeping profusely and told him about his son's death. The Brahmin Sunanda asked his to chant the eleventh canto of the Gita and then throw votive water on his son's dead body and would get his son relive. The city man did so and got back his son live. Amazed he wanted to know about this demon and was told: 'In earlier life that demon was a farmer. In his farm, a willing was devouring a human but the farmer didn't look towards that. However, some other Brahmin ran to save the person, making the vulture fly back top the stay. The Brahmin (second one) whereupon gave the first one the curse to become a demon. Now that demon used to consume one of us everyday. We decided to sacrifice one of us voluntarily to save the trouble for all. It was that demon who killed your friends, but you could survive become you need the eleventh canto of the Gita everyday.' Hearing this Sunanda threw the votive water upon his friends' body and they also got up, alive and kicking. This way chanting or the reading of the eleventh canto ensures safety from the evil forces.

(xii) **Twelfth canto:** Once a prince happened to come in Kolhapur city and going at the Manikarna teertha offered water-oblation to his departed father. He had also propitiated goddess Mahalakshmi, who appeared before him and asked him to have his boon. In the response, the prince said: 'O goddess! My father fell ill and expired. In the meanwhile, the consecrated horse was stolen, which I am unable to find out.' The goddess suggested a way to find the horse and told the prince: 'Just before my temple's gate dwells there a *Siddha* Brahmin called Siddhi Samadhi. I shall instruct him and he shall do the needful for you.'

As the goddess replied the prince to have gone to the Brahmin and told him all that he heard from the goddess. The Brahmin whereupon suggested summoning the horse by the power of the mantra. The gods came before them when the Brahmin used the mantra power. The Siddha Brahmin asked Indra to instruct gods to find the lost horse of the prince. Sooner, the horse was found. This surprised the prince who said: 'I have not yet cremated my father and his body is lying in the pool of oil. He could be revived by your mantra power, he may complete unfinished Ashwamedha Yajna.' The Brahmin agreed. The prince took the Brahmin to the venue of the yajna and made the Brahmin sprinkle holy water on to his father's oil soaked body. His father, the king was instantly revived back to life. When the amazed prince asked the Brahmin, the secret of his mantra-power, he told, 'I have been chanting the twelfth canto of Srimadh Bhagwatgita for many years. It is the chanting that developed this dead reviving power in his mantra. The prince decided to do the same. Such is the power one gets it one every day reads the twelfth canto of Bhagwat Gita.

(xiii) **Thirteenth Canto:** The consequence of reading this canto of Bhagavadgita makes one involved in views and bad habits getting redemption quickly. Narrating the story, lord Shiva highlighted the glory of reading this canto this way.

Long ago, there lived a Brahmin named Hari Dikhit on the banks of the river Tungabhadra. Her wife was of very evil temperament. All the time, she remained involved in vices. She loved to have physical contact with other persons even while neglecting her husband . One night, she was waiting for her lover in a quiet jungle, when a tiger attacked her. She then told the beast that a person longing for sex should never be attacked. The beast whereupon said that in previous life he was also a Brahmin and in the lure of money he used to perform yajna for the most wicked persons. Not only that he would usurp other's share in the yajna itself 'Since, I was very greedy, I got ino this species in my present life. And now in this life, I may let go the noble natured persons but never a wicked person.' So, saying the beast reduced that women to pieces and ate her up. After her death the woman had to languish in a variety of hells. Eventually, she became a pariah woman and was afflicted with scores of diseases. One day while roaming aimlessly, she happened to reach Hariharapur and had the *darshan* of a Brahmin named Vasudeva. That Brahmin read the thirteenth canto of Bhagavadgita every day. As she heard that Brahmin chant the thirteenth canto she was redeemed from miserable existence and went to heaven.

(xiv) **Fourteenth Canto:** In the very beginning, there was a king called Betaal in Singhal Dweep (modern Lanka). He had a bitch whom he loved very much. Once, he went for hunting and let his hitch chase a rabbit. Running for life, the rabbit happened to reach that jungle in which beasts and smaller animals coexist, forgetting their antipathy. It was due to a great samaritan called Mahatma Vatsa. He used to read the fourteenth canto of Bhagavadgita every day without fail. That fleeing rabbit happened to reach near him and fell before his feet. Coincidently, the bitch also came there where he used to wash his feet. A small puddle of water was created. The rabbit and the bitch fell in that puddle together and expired. As they fell, both of them, by his grace, chanted the fourteenth canto of Bhagavadgita, attained salvation.

The king happened to reach there and was surprised to see the arch enemy attaining salvation together. But the disciples of the great sage-mahatma Vatsa-told the king that it was due to the sage reading the fourteenth canto everyday. Listening this recilation, even the arch enemies become bosom friends. The king all stopped hunting and began to chant the fourteenth canto Bhagavadgita.

(xv) **Fifteen Canto:** Telling the related tale to this canto Lord Shiva told Parvati that there was a very brave and chivalrous king Nrisingh in the state called Gaurha. He had a wicked commander, who nursed an ambition of killing his king and the princes and becoming the king himself. He fell ill and died before he could implement his plans. Since the crime had been mentally committed, he took his next birth as a horse. That horse was very sturdy and good looking. A trader purchased that horse and curiously enough, sold to none else but Raja Nrisingh. One day, the king went for hunting astride that very horse as his had luck would have it, his entourage trailed behind. The king was very thirsty and hungry. He tied his horse beneath a tree and went ahead in search of water; while searching for water he happened to find a big leaf inscribed with first shloka of Bhagavadgita's fifteenth canto. As he chanted the shloka, his horse died instantly and attained salvation ----amazed, the king moved ahead and found a sage Vishnu Sharma. Chanting the fifteenth canto of the Bhagavadgita. When the king told him about his horse's death, Vishnu Sharma told him the reason behind that horse's instant death. Having learnt about the cause, the king developed surfeit from the natural riches and appointed his son as the king, left for jungle, where be chanted the fiffteenth canto. Eventually, the king also attained salvation.

(xvi) **Sixteenth Canto:** Highlighting the chanting of this canto of the Bhagavadgita, lord Shankara related another story to Parvati, which is as follows.

There was a king called Khadagbahu in the city of Saurashtra. He had an elephant called Arimardan. Once that elephant went berserk and created much disturbance. In a maddened frenzy, it ran across the street and no one could dare stop it. It created a panick to the residents nearby. The king got this news and came there with sons, but seeing that pachyderm's craze, nobody could dare go near the elephant. At that time, a Brahmin came chanting some mantra and happened to pass close to the elephant. Although, people tried to stop him, the brahmin kept on moving undaunted. Suddenly, all saw the elephant behaving like a tamed dog. When the king asked as to how that Brahmin could show his miracle, the Brahmin said: 'I was chanting the sixteenth canto of Bhagavadgita. Perhaps, it is due to the influence of that chant.' The king then liberally honoured that brahmin and started to learn that canto from the Brahmin. Subsequently, the king dwelt peacefully and on his death, he also attained salvation.

(xvii) **Seventeenth Canto:** Highlighting the importance of this canto of Bhagavadgita, Lord Shiva told Parvati another story. In olden times, there was a king called

Khadga Singh. He had a very recalcitrant son named Dushyasan who used to torture people sitting upon his elephant. One day he happened to slip from his seat on the elephant and was eventually trampled under foot. In the next life he was borm as an elephant himself. Khadga Singh had this elephant sent to him by his friend the king of Singhal dweep. Khadga Singh didn't keep this elephant and gifted to a poet, who sold off this elephant to another king. The elephant expired after sometime. The elephant had been afflicted with many ailments and died in a pathetic condition. Before its death, Khadga Singh brought the best physician to have the elephant treated. But, the pachyderm said: 'I won't be cured by medicines. I am sure to die. Please arrange for some Brahmin versed in Vedas (Ved-Paathi), to recite the sevetneenth canto of Bhagavadgita.' The king did so and that elephant expired. The king learnt from the Brahmin the effect of reciting the seventeenth canto of Bhagavadgita. He also learnt it and began to chant himself every day. Eventually, he attained salvation. It is believed that recitation of seventeen ensures peaceful death.

(xviii) **Eighteenth Canto:** Lord Shankar said to Parvati: "O moon-faced: The eighteenth and final canto of Bhagavadgita destroys ignorance and ensures one's redemption from worldly tortures. I will tell you a story, which highlights the importance of this canto.

Once Indra was seated on his throne in Amaravati, when some couriers of lord Vishnu came and removed Indra from the exalted throne and made another person ascend it. As that successor occupied the throne of the divine chief, the Apsaras came along with gandharvas-kinnars and began to entertain the successor Indra. The displaced Indra thought that this person must have been meritorious enough to get such coveted honour. Indra then went to lord Vishnu and expressed his curiosity, 'You allowed me to occupy this throne after I had accomplished more than 100 Ashwamedha yajnas. What did the person do to get this exalted throne?' Lord Vishnu said : 'Indra! This person had performed no Ashwamedha yajnas, but did beyond that. He had read the nineteenth canto of Bhagavadgita every day during stay in the mortal world. Hence, he got your throne. You can also do the same to get back your lost throne.'

Getting this instruction, Indra went straight to the river Godavari and learnt the eighteenth canto from a learned Brahmin. While chanting the eighteenth canto of Bhagavadgita, Indra realized the great peace that he experienced. He eventually got back his lost throne.

Having told Parvati the importance of eighteen cantoes of Bhagavadgita, lord Shankara further said: 'The Bhagavadgita epitomizes the entire essence of the Scriptures. It has the gist of the Upanishads and the essence of Vedas. It is that nectar that makes the listener live in communion with eternity. It tells the being what should one do to stay away from the travails of the worldly existence. It is the discourse that is revealed by the super God himself. If the entire Scriptures are likened to a cow, the Bhagavadgita is the ghee made from the milk given by that cow.'

5. Raja Dilip and Nandini Cow

Hearing about the Bhagavadgita, all the sages felt unprovenly thrilled. They said with reference to the cow : "O great sage Vyasji! We have heard that in the solar dynasty there was a Raja, named Dilip who even tried to sacrifice his own life to save a cow's life. Please tell this episode in details.' Vyasji then narrated the following story.

Raja Dilip was born in Vaivaswata Manu's lineage and was a renowned king of the solar dynasty. Although, he had everything he longed for a son. One day, he went to his family priest Vasishtha and revealed his agony. He said: 'Even though I have every comfort, why I have no heir. It is due to any curse for the misdeed, I might have committed unknowingly: 'Yes, O king, once you were returning to earth after meeting the divine chief Indra. You were in such a great hurry that you happened to neglect the divine cow, Kaamadhenu. She took the insult to her heart and cursed that since you had not taken the dust from her cow and neither circumambulated around her, you may be devoid of a son. Now, you can make good of this lapse, I have a cow Nandini, who is actually the daughter of Kaamdhenu. Now if you render devoted service to her, you may have Kaamdhenu take back her curse.'

Raja Dilip gratefully accepted the offer and began to render a devoted service to Nandini. He would look after her every need. The king would be all the time he was closer to Nandini. One day, the cow Nandini happened to reach atop hill while wandering and enjoying the natural pulchritude. Dilip was behind her That spot had such an enchanting view of nature that even Dilip was left spell bound. Nandini kept on moving ahead. Suddenly, the dreadful lion approached her, seeing which Nandini bellowed in panic. Raja Dilip saw the approaching lion and readied his bow and arrow. Suddenly, his body became stiff and immobile. The lion whereupon said: 'O king! You can't kill me in this jungle. In fact, I am one of the hench person of lord Shiva. Mother Parvati had permitted me to eat in this jungle, whatever I went. It is by her that loon that your hand and body become immobile and stiff.'

But Dilip requested the lion. 'All right, you may have whatever you want. I request you that instead of devouring this holy cow, you should better eat me up. It is my vow to save this cow Nandini at all costs.' And saying so, Dilip just bowed down, ready to be devoured by the lion. All of a sudden, Dilip had flowers naming on him. He opened his eyes he found the lion absent and Nandini smiling. 'Get up, King. You have succeeded in your test. That lion was created by my illusive power. I am satisfied with your devotion. My mother, Kaamdhenu has agreed to take back her curse. Now you will get a renowned son.'

It was Dilip's son Raghu, who became such a famous king. Concluding the tab, Vyasji said: 'One should never neglect a cow or Brahmin, no matter how busy one may be.'

6. Different forms of Super Gods

Not the sages asked Vyasji that why our three super gods have different representative iconic images. 'Why lord Shiva is represented by the lingam, Why lord Vishnu has four hands and wary Brahma remains rater comparatively unadorned?"

Replying to their query, Vyasji told the sages that once this question was raised in a huge assembly of sages as to who was the super god, deserving most adoration. The great sage Bhrigu decided to find this answer. He first went to lord Shiva's realm, but was denied entry, because lord was enjoying copulation with consort Parvati. Enraged, Bhrigu left cursing lord Shiva, said: 'Since copulation to you is the most important act, I curse that you will be known not by your actual form, but by your *lingam* (phallus).'

He then went to lord Brahma's realm, but Brahma paid just no attention to Bhrigu. Bhrigu cursed the creator: 'Since, you become indifferent to your creation after doing your job and don't care what is good or bad, you will also be shown equal indifference by your creation. You will be adored or worshipped very rarely and that too in the company of other gods.'

Now Bhrigu went to Vaikuntha to meet lord Vishnu. The lord was asleep, but Bhrigu went straight to his bed chamber. Reaching there, he kicked lord Vishnu on the latter's bossom, saying 'While the people are restive and full of agony, you are having your beauty-sleep.' Lord Vishnu at once woke up and rubbing Bhrigu's kicking foot softly, said apologetically: 'I am sorry great sage that when you came I was asleep. I shall now be more vigilant to look after people's welfare.'

This humility of Vishnu made Bhrigu to reply: 'O great lord! Henceforth, I declare that you will be the most worshipped deity on the earth and at once most powerful.' It is believed that since then lord Vishnu had four arms, which symbolisied his added power.

7. Kriya Yoga Saar
[Essence of Human Actions]

Bhishma sought Pulastya: 'O great sage! I am extremely fortunate to have listened so many enlightening tales from you. Tell me what should be the ultimate aim of any action by man. What is that destination towards which all beings should aim?'

Pulastya replied: 'All must try to win lord Vishnu's grace. That is the final aim. Because, if one has lord Vishnu's favour, everything else in the world becomes easily accessible to one. Remember that lord Vishnu is the ultimate deity. He is not only the sustainer, but verily the creator and destroyer, as well. For, Brahma and Shiva act only at His implying. Listening His tales, is incarnation and believing in their efficacy is some means of liberation for beings. He is the Purush with whose contact could mingle with Prakriti, life gets created. Worship him or any of His forms, for only that can give liberation or emancipation from this world's mortal travails He is the one, who resolves to create the world and the world gets created. It is He, who masters Time and its divisions. All Satya, Treta, Dwapar, and Kaliyug move in their fixed pattern by His order. While it is easier to have his darshan in Satya Yuga and progressively more difficult in the subsequent Ages, each age has its merit scale. In Satya Yuga, one gets little merit even after performing thousands of yajna, and treat hundreds and in Dwapara this, but in Kali Yuga even a day's devoted worship may give the devotee a merit equivalent to the performance of a thousand yajnas in Satya Yuga. Although, Kali Yuga is full of difficulties, it has this great advantage. So, worship lord Vishnu and ensure salvation."

Bhishma was thrilled on the Pulastya's sermon. He bade adieu and left for his abode. This completes the *Padma Purana*. Readers or listeners will get special favour from lord Vishnu.

❑ ❑ ❑

HEALTH BOOKS

Yoga Guru Sunil Singh
Healing through Yoga
Dr. Shalini Chakrabarty
Handbook on Diabetes
Handbook on High Blood Pressure
Jayashree Thatte Bhat
Journey Through Breast Cancer
Arlene Normand
The Ten Commandment of Losing Weights
Ted Andrew
How to Heal with Colour
Nancy Mramor
Spritual Fitness
Aladar Kogler
Yoga for Every Athlete
Srikantha Arunachalam
Treatise on Ayurveda
David Servan Schriber (Guerir)
The Instinct to Heal
M. Subramaniam
Unveiling the Secrets of Reiki
Brilliant Light
At the Feet of the Master (Manal Reiki)
Sukhdeepak Malvai
Natural Healing with Reiki
Pt.Rajnikant Upadhayay
Reiki
Mudra Vigyan (For Health & Happiness)
Sankalpo
Neo Reiki
Dr. Shiv Kumar
Aroma Therapy
Causes, Cure & Prevention of Nervous Disease
Diseases of Digestive System
Asthma-Allergies (Causes & Cure)
Eye-Care (Without Glassess)
Stress
Dr. Satish Goel
Causes & Cure of Blood Pressure
Causes & Cure of Diabetes
Causes & Cure of Heart Ailments
Pregnancy & Child Care
Ladies Slimming Course
Acupuncture Guide
Acupressure Guide
Acupuncture & Acupressure Guide
Walking for Better Health
Nature Cure for Health & Happiness
A Beacon of Hope for the Childless Couples
Dr. Kanta Gupta
Be Your Own Doctor
Dr. M.K. Gupta
Causes, Cure & Prevention
of High Blood Cholesterol
Acharya Bhagwan Dev
Yoga for Better Health
Pranayam, Kundalini aur Hathyoga
Asha Pran
Beauty Guide (With Make-up Guide)
Acharya Vipul Rao
Ayurvedic Treatment for Common Diseases
Herbal Treatment for Common Diseases
Dr. Ashok Gupta
Naturopathy for Better Health
Juice Therapy for Better Health
Acharya Satyanand
Surya Chikitsa
G. D. Budhiraja
Healthy Aging
Bharti Taneja
Skin So Beautifully Yours
Dr. Pushpa Khurana
Be Young and Healthy for 100 Years
The Awesome Challenge of AIDS

Dr. S.K. Sharma
Add Inches
Shed Weight Add Life
Alternate Therapies
Miracles of Urine Thserapy
Meditation & Dhyan Yoga
A Complete Guide to Homeopathic Remedies
A Complete Guide to Biochemic Remedies
Common Diseases of Urinary System
Alopathic Guide for Common Disorders 1
Wonders of Magnetotherapy
Family Homeopathic Guide
Health in Your Hands
Food for Good Health
Juice Therapy
Dr. Renu Gupta
Hair Care (Prevention of Dandruff & Baldness)
Skin Care
Complete Beautician Course
Common Diseases of Women
Dr. Rajiv Sharma
Grand's Ma Home Tips
First Aid
Causes, Cure and Prevention
of Children's Diseases
Message for God Health
Diet Management Guide   1
Exercise Management Guide   1
Mouth, Teeth & Ear-Nose Throat Disorder
M. Kumaria
How to Keep Fit
Dr. Nishtha
Diseases of Respiratory Tract
(Nose, Throat, Chest & Lungs)
Backache (Spondylitis, Cervical, Arthrtis Rheumatism)
Ladies Health Guide (With Make-up Guide)
Manoj Kumar
Diamond Body Building Course
Koulacharya Jagdish Sharma
Body Language   1
G.C. Goyal
Vitamins for Natural Healing
Dr. Vishnu Jain
Heart to Heart (with Heart Specialist)
Dr. Sajiv Adlakha
Stuttering & Your Child (Question-Answer)
Dr. L. R. Chaudhary
Rajuvenate Kundalini Mantra Yoga
Dr. Rekhaa Kale
Easy Guide to Meditation
Easy Guide To Relationship Building
Easy Guide to Reiki
Easy Guide to Peace of Mind
Easy Guide to Feng Sui
Easy Guide to Dowsing
Past Life

Sex Education Series
Dayanand Verma
Sex- A New Concept
Om Gupta
How to Enjoy Sex (Questions & Answer)
Dr. S.K. Sharma
Tips on Sex
Dr. Rajiv Sharma
New Kamsutra (Sex Management Guide)
Dr. B.R. Kishore
Vatsyanana Kamasutra
The Manual of Sex & Tantra
Dr. K.Sohail & Bette Davis
Love Sex & Marriage
Dr. Satish Goel
Sex For All

⊚ **DIAMOND BOOKS** X-30, Okhla Industrial Area, Phase-II, New Delhi-110020,
Phone : 011-40712100, Fax : 011-41611866, E-mail : sales@dpb.in, Website : www.dpb.in

Religion and Spirituality

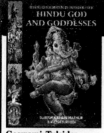

Goswami Tulsidas
- ❑ Sri Ramcharitmanasa (Doha- Chopai in Hindi, Roman Description in English) ....

Ed. Acharya Bhagwan Dev
- ❑ Sanskar Vidhi ....

B.K. Chaturvedi
- ❑ Gods & Goddesses of India ....
- ❑ Shiv Purana ....
- ❑ Vishnu Purana ....
- ❑ Shrimad Bhagvat Purana ....
- ❑ Devi Bhagvat Purana ....
- ❑ Garud Purana ....
- ❑ Agni Purana ....
- ❑ Varah Purana ....
- ❑ Brahamvevart Purana ....
- ❑ The Hymns & Orisons of Lord Shiva (Roman) ....
- ❑ Sri Hanuman Chalisa (Roman) ....
- ❑ Pilgrimage Centres of India ....
- ❑ Chalisa Sangreh ....

S. K. Sharma
- ❑ The Brilliance of Hinduism ....,..
- ❑ Sanskar Vidhi (Arya Samaj) ....

Dr. B.R. Kishore
- ❑ Hinduism ....
- ❑ Rigveda ....
- ❑ Samveda ....
- ❑ Yajurveda ...,...................
- ❑ Atharvveda ....
- ❑ Mahabharata ....
- ❑ Ramayana ....
- ❑ Supreme Mother Goddeses Durga (4 Colour Durga Chalisa) ....

Manish Verma
- ❑ Fast & Festivals of India ....

Prof. Gurpret Singh
- ❑ Soul of Sikhism ....

Shiv Sharma
- ❑ Soul of Jainism ....

Pt. Ramesh Tiwari
- ❑ Shrimad Bhagavad Gita (Krishna, the Charioteer) (Sanskrit, Hindi, English & Description in English) ....

Manan Sharma
- ❑ Buddhism (Teachings of Buddha) ....
- ❑ Universality of Buddha ....

Anurag Sharma
- ❑ Life Profile & Biography of Buddha .....
- ❑ Thus Spoke Buddha ....

Udit Sharma
- ❑ Teachings & Philosophy of Buddha .....

S.P. Ojha
- ❑ Sri-Ram-Charit Manas ....

Chakor Ajgaonkar
- ❑ Realm of Sadhana (What Saints & Masters Say) ....

K.H. Nagrani
- ❑ A Child from the Spirit World Speaks ....

F.S. Growse
- ❑ Mathura & Vrindavan, The Mystical Land of Lord Krishna (8 Colour photos) ....

Dr. Giriraj Shah
- ❑ Glory of Indian Culture ....

R.P. Hingorani
- ❑ Chalisa Sangreh (Roman) ....

Acharya Vipul Rao
- ❑ Srimad Bhagwat Geeta (Sanskrit & English) ....

Dr. Bhavansingh Rana
- ❑ 108 Upanishad (In press) ....

Eva Bell Barer
- ❑ Quiet Talks with the Master ....

Joseph J. Ghosh
- ❑ Adventures with Evil Spirits ....

Dr. S.P. Ruhela
- ❑ Fragrant Spiritual Memories of a Karma Yogi ....

Yogi M.K. Spencer
- ❑ Rishi Ram Ram ....
- ❑ Oneness with God ....

H. Seereeram
- ❑ Fundamentals of Hinduism ....

Books in Roman
- ❑ Bhajan, Lokgeet or Aartiyan (Roman English, Hindi) ....
- ❑ Hindu Vrat Kathayen (Including Saptvaar Vrat Kathayen) ......
- ❑ Chalisa Sangreh (Including Aarties in Roman) ....
- ❑ Shri Satya Narayana Vrat Katha (In English and Hindi) ....
- ❑ Sanatan Dharm Poojā ....
- ❑ Sudha Kalp ....
- ❑ Shiv Abhisek Poojan ....
- ❑ Daily Prayer (Hindi, English, French, Roman)
- ❑ Sanatan Daily Prayer ....
- ❑ Durga Chalisa ....,.....................
- ❑ Gaytari Chalisa ....,.........
- ❑ Shiv Chalisa ....
- ❑ Hanuman Chalisa ....

Acharya Vipul Rao
- ❑ Daily Prayer ....

Books can be requisitioned by V.P.P. Postage charges will be Rs. 20/- per book. For orders of three books the postage will be free.

✪ DIAMOND POCKET BOOKS

X-30, Okhla Industrial Area, Phase-II, New Delhi-110020, Phone : 011-51611861, Fax : 011-51611866
E-mail : sales@diamondpublication.com, Website : www.fusionbooks.com

Divine Gems

Message of Upanishads
Dr. B. B. Paliwal

Upanishads are the epitome of eternal knowledge. They form the treasure-trove of the sacred Vedic philosophy. Upanishads are the beacon light of all spiritual knowledge dealing with the universe and life—about creation, birth and death as well as time and space. The whole existence revolves around this eternal truth which is the metaphysical tenet of life. This knowledge is delineated in a comprehensible format in this book for the common readers. Upanishads are the gift of India to the entire

Message of Vedas
Dr. B. B. Paliwal

In the common parlance 'Vedas' means 'knowledge'. These sacred tomes are the beacon lights of enlightenment which dispel the darkness of ignorance from the human minds. The trove of ancient Indian philosophy and culture. The mysteries of the universe, creation and existence, the time-space relationship all such metaphysical tenets are delineated in the Vedas. This book is an attempt to simplify the intriguing tenets of the Vedas into a comprehensive version for the benefit of the common readers.

Message of Purans
Dr. B. B. Paliwal

In the Purans, the story of creation has been delineated in great detail. Purans are the timeless tomes of the secrets of the universe and life—about the mysterious dimensions of time and space—about the animate and the inanimate as well as about the flora and the fauna. The Purans tell you what happened in the past, what is happening in the present and what will happen in the future.

: BOOKS FOR CHILDREN :

B. K. Chaturvedi
Tales from Ramayan .....
Tales from the Vedas .....
Mahesh Sharma
Tales from Mahabhart .....
Tales from Puranas .....
Tales from the Upanishads .....

Books can be requisitioned by V.P.P. Postage charges will be Rs. 20/- per book. For orders of three books the postage will be free.

⊙ DIAMOND POCKET BOOKS (P.) Ltd.
X-30, Okhla Industrial Area, Phase-II, Phone : 011-41611861-5, Fax : 011-41611866
E-mail : sales@diamondpublication.com, Website : www.diamondpublication.com